The History of the Knowledge of London

LONDON TAXI KNOWLEDGE

Philip Warren

Published by London Publishing Company

First Published May 2003

Copyright © 2003 DJA Design Limited
ISBN 0-9545131-0-X

London Publishing Company Limited
15 Harewood Avenue
London NW1 6LE
020 7493 5267
www.thecabdriver.com

All rights owned by
DJA Design Limited

Artwork & Design
DJA Design Limited

Illustrations
Walter Lowe @
DJA Design Limited

Photographs
Supplied by Philip Warren

Printed in Great Britain by
Chandlers Printers Limited
Saxon Mews, Reginald Road
Bexhill on Sea, East Sussex TN39 3PJ
Tel: 01424 212684
Fax: 01424 225878

Introduction

Philip Warren became a licensed London taxi driver in January 1956, taking nine months to do the knowledge. He had joined a trade in which his grandfather had joined in 1888 and his father in 1927. Philip handed in his licence in 1998. He was a member of the Crisis Committee in 1961 following the introduction of minicabs in June of that year.

He later joined the T & GWU and in 1974 became chairman of the Cab Trade Committee. He had been editor of Cab Trade News since February 1972. He left the Union in 1975. Later that year he was offered the position as editor of Steering Wheel. He resigned from that position in the middle of 1977 because of disagreement with the new owner, an East End scrap metal merchant! He is again editing Steering Wheel since the take over by London Publishing in 1987, headed by Dave Allen.

He had been researching the history of the London cab trade when he discovered that the trade had first been licensed by an Act of Oliver Cromwell, in June 1654 under the control of the Court of Aldermen in the City of London.

In 1991 he was one one of the original founders of the Company of Hackney Carriage Drivers and he had the distinction of being Master, when the 300 year old cab trade celebrated the event with a banquet at the Guildhall in the City of London.

Other distinctions include co-writing with Malcolm Linskey 'Taxicabs A Photographic History' published in 1976 and a second edition in 1980. In 1984 he assisted in the publication of a book commemorating the 75th anniversary of the London General Cab Company Ltd. He also reflects on joining Mann & Overton in 1980 and the benefits he gained working in close collaboration with their MD, Peter Wildgoose. Philip also reflects on the kindness of Mann & Overton Ltd, following his leaving in 1986, to take care of his wife, who was suffering from Alzheimer's Disease, until she died in 1992.

Several other distinctions stand out, organising for several years the Trade Exhibitions in Battersea Park, the presentation to the Public Carriage Office, of the lineage of control of the cab trade from 1654 and another great moment of pride when his son Timothy became a London licensed taxi driver in 1993. It was the publication of Philip's Magnum Opus- The History of the London Cab Trade in 1995 which vindicated many years of research and the patience of his late wife.

The picture shows a group of 'knowledge boys' outside the British Legion's Knowledge School in Harleyford Street, Kennington Oval in July 1956. The author, Philip Warren, is standing between Mr Steadman the Superintendent of the school and Alec Lardent, the school's instructor with outstretched hand. Alec Lardent was famous for his throw away line "let the cotton be a guide but don't let it strangle you."

4

Chapter One

For two days labour, you ask for 200 guineas?
No, I ask it for the knowledge of a lifetime.
(Whistler)

The early history of the Knowledge of London has remained a mystery to many thousands of London's taxi drivers. They know what it is and what it takes to achieve it. I am sure that it takes a special kind of man and woman to complete what is definitely the most difficult study required to join what is obviously a working class trade.

I would go further and say that it is the equivalent of a three year university study and the license obtained by those who have stayed the course, and more fail than pass, compares with a degree at the lower echelon universities. Further, this is not a degree that can be gained by studying in the ambience of a university, but must be gained, riding a moped in the dangers of London's heavy traffic, followed by hours of map and notes study, committing to memory, what has been learned riding through the maze of London's streets.

This is not a story which details how the 'knowledge' is carried out, but a history of when it started and how it has progressed until modern times. It is only a few years, in terms of how long the 'knowledge' has been a requirement, that there are now women taxi drivers but, the intrigue which prevented their earlier licensing is almost unbelievable.

A VERY OLD
TYPE TAXI :
(VERY OLD ! !)

Left: The Prunel, introduced into London in 1903 was the first internal combustion engine vehicle to operate as a cab, only one vehicle was licensed. The driver was James Howe, who, in August 1933 was presented with a special badge, No.1, by Lord Trenchard, then Commissioner of Police, at Scotland Yard. This badge now hangs with others at the Public Carriage Office.

Below: The Bersey electrically propelled cab was introduced in 1897, the design of Mr.C.W.Bersey. They only operated for about two years from a garage in Juxon Street, off Lambeth Road.

The answer to the intriguing question when did the 'knowledge' start proved to be very elusive. Prior to 1869, when the annual Metropolitan Police Reports were first published in book form, the reports dating from 1843, when the Commissioner of Police became involved in hackney carriages, were published in Parliamentary Papers. These revealed nothing at all about the 'knowledge.'

Success eventually came when, after checking all the Reports from 1869 to 1883, it was in the Report for 1888 that I struck gold! I had been unable to trace reports from 1884 to 1887 but the 1888 Report gave information back to 1884. Headed thus:-

KNOWLEDGE EXAMINATIONS

2,316 men were examined, 318 more than in 1887, 855 failed the exam.

Whence cometh the knowledge? (obscure origins)

Year	Passed	Failed
1884	1,214	717
1885	1,219	601
1886	1,328	545
1887	1,357	579
1888	1,461	855

The Report stated: "This examination as to the 'knowledge' is limited to principal streets and squares and public buildings. Applicants for the ''knowledge' were all generally of the same class, ie persons who had a knowledge of horses."

There was no driving test for horse drawn cabs and a certificate signed by two competent people, ie, doctor, parson or bank official etc; was considered adequate proof that the applicant could drive a horse drawn carriage.

As far as it is possible to ascertain the Public Carriage Office was first mentioned as a separate entity in the Commissioner's Report for 1885. These early reports gave other interesting information, for example, the 1888 report listed all 38 cab shelters (see appendix). The cabs were inspected mainly at night by inspectors in plain clothes from the Public Carriage Office and in 1885 the report stated that 252 Hansoms and 127 Growlers were reported, of these 21 were declared unfit for use as were four horses.

Rewards for handing in lost property did not commence until 1870. In 1869 only 1,912 articles were handed in,but in 1873 the numbers had risen to 14,136 and apart from the reward for claimed articles, unclaimed items were given to the drivers as they are today. In 1876 there were 15,680 items handed in, among these were a bag of jewellery valued at £1,000, a case containing £1,000 of Bank of England notes and a diamond necklace also valued at £1,000. The drivers were rewarded!

FIGURES FOR LOST PROPERTY OVER TEN YEARS

1869	1,912
1870	3,258
1871	7,709
1872	12,950
1873	14,136
1874	14,076
1875	15,584
1876	15,680
1877	15,726
1878	16,564
1879	15,514
1880	16,849

The estimated value for the last five years was £1,000,000 and in 1895 one driver was rewarded with £75 for handing in a bag of gold valued at £700. In 1896 there were 38,025 items handed in of which 19,461 were returned to the losers. The items handed in included artificial teeth, a live parrot, 5 larks in a cage, cases of stuffed birds, cats and dogs, a live rabbit, a suit of armour, a large number of books, bicycles, cyclometers, a galvanometer, swords, revolvers, a perambulator, several mail carts (children's toys) sewing machines, golf clubs and various musical instruments.

Taxi drivers have often wondered how passengers could leave items in the back of the cab, some are quite valuable, but how could passengers manage to forget a live parrot, a bicycle and a suit of armour in a horse drawn cab? Just imagine, getting the armour in would have been difficult, the noise of metal on metal, the passenger would have needed help they would have had to listen to ribald remarks from passing members of the public, such as: "Where are you going, Agincourt? or "The Battle of Hastings is over mate!" At least one of the swords would have been complimentary to the armour, but a revolver!

The Report for 1888 listed details of cabs and drivers back to 1884 thus:-

Year	Cabs	Drivers
1884	12,905	13,824
1885	13,151	14,252
1886	13,548	14,852
1887	13,996	15,100
1888	14,247	15,514

The Commissioner's Report for 1889 revealed that 1,219 applicants passed the 'knowledge'and the report stated that examinations now extend to several railway stations, principle streets, squares and public buildings. In 1892 there was a further change in the ''knowledge' procedure, as well as the former locations drivers were now asked "the most expeditious routes to and from these various locations.

A return for Knowledge of London examinations from January 1st 1884 to May 1st inclusive, showed that 333 passed, 76 were rejected once and subsequently were re-examined and passed. Seventeen applicants were examined four times before passing and nine applicants made five appearances before passing. This was a total of 435 examined over a period of five months.

Prior to 1896, the only examination which cab drivers were subjected to and had been since 1884, was the Knowledge of London. There was no driving test for motor cab drivers until 1907 and the ''knowledge' questions were quite simple, such as: Scotland Yard to Paddington Station, from Paddington to the Bank and from the Bank to Sidney Street, Chelsea. All the starting points and the destinations were those that a cab driver would require to know during his day to day work.

During 1894, 1,205 persons made appearances for the 'knowledge' prior to being licensed as cab drivers. Of the number who did pass, many were examined more than once and in some cases as many as six appearances were made. If we take a year at random nearer to our own time, for example 1976, there were 2,938 first time appearances and a total of 19,869 attendances, yet only 588 got their requisition. There is no record when those who passed started the 'knowledge' but many must have started in 1975 or even earlier. Of those 588 who did pass 121 were yellow badge (suburban) and 18 suburban drivers took the full London license.

From a high of drivers licensed in 1891 there had been a steady decrease up to 1895, as shown.

Year	Numbers licensed
1891	15,219
1892	15,011
1893	14,985
1894	14,672
1985	13,498

The number of newly licensed drivers were not replacing those who had left the trade. This in part may have been due to the raising of the age limit from 18 to 21. There was also the first criticisms that the 'knowledge' was too difficult.

Until about 1900 some 95 per cent of London was contained within a four mile circle of Charing Cross. Only in the East was there expansion as far as Stratford and that was only a fairly narrow corridor. In the middle to late 19th century London extended South to Camberwell Green, to Camden Town in the North and in the West to Maida Vale. Vauxhall was in the country as was Battersea, Brixton was a small village as were Kilburn, Highgate, Stamford Hill, Stoke Newington, Chelsea and Clapham. Taking London as a whole four fifths of the town lay north of the Thames.

There was a good reason why the expansion of London south of the Thames was late in development. Three new bridges across the Thames had been built between 1816 and 1819, they were Vauxhall, Waterloo and Southwark bridges. Unfortunately all these bridges carried a toll of a 1/2d for pedestrians which meant that a labourer living south of the river would have been required to pay the equivalent of a weeks wages for the right to walk to work, during the course of a year

Southwark Bridge was the first bridge to be freed of toll when the City Corporation purchased the bridge for £218,868 and gave it to the public "free of tolls for ever". Lambeth, Vauxhall, Chelsea Albert and Battersea bridges were not made free of tolls until 1879. Even then expansion south of the Thames was slow.

In July 1895 the Public Carriage Office was substantially increased, both in numbers of staff and the number of passing stations from six to ten, each with an inspector, a sergeant and constable. This it was claimed would lead to a more effective supervision over horses and cabs and did lead to an improvement in both.

Also in 1895 the name Lost Property Office appeared for the first time in the Commissioners Reports, though no particular significance can be attached to that, except that lost property in cabs and buses had grown considerably. The amount of business transacted at this office during 1895 showed a considerable increase over the preceding years thus:-

1892 there were 27,230 items deposited
1893   "   " 26,788   "   "
1894   "   " 29,716   "   "
1895   "   " 32,997   "   "

Articles deposited in 1895 included 2,499 purses, 759 articles of jewellery, 160 gold and silver watches, 2,306 bags many containing items of value, 734 opera and field glasses, 15,626 umbrellas and walking sticks, 280 rugs and 7,364 miscellaneous articles.

Among the latter was £700 in a bankers bag, a telescope, bicycles, a bantam cock, a cat, a canary in a cage, cylinders of compressed gas, rifles, guns, a sewing machine, stage props a suit of chain mail (probably the same man who had previously left a suit of armour in a cab) and various tools. Items left in buses are also included in the above but as there were nearly four times as many cabs as there were buses, it would be fair to say that the majority of items were left in cabs.

In 1896 there were 1,645 applicants for a cab driver's license, set out from the Commissioners Report as below:-

Month	Attended	Passed	Failed
January	91	73	18
February	83	51	32
March	116	82	34
April	98	81	17
May	84	59	25
June	69	42	27
July	90	63	27
August	88	58	30
September	174	98	76
October	270	172	98
November	254	136	118
December	228	143	85

We do not know how the appearances were conducted, whether on weekly, fortnightly or a monthly basis. In the same year places of amusement were added to the questions asked but it appears not to have added materially to the time taken to do the 'knowledge'. No reason was given as to why the applicants for the last four months were double those of the preceding eight.

For the first time the Commissioner's Report referred to a driving test and that of the 1,058 who passed the 'knowledge', 67 failed the driving test, though an unspecified number passed after several tests.

One interesting fact emerged from the 1896 report. In 220 cases the Commissioner declined to renew the licenses of men who, after a previous caution had either failed to use their license at all, or, had only used them for a short period. These men the report stated are known as 'Butterflies', because they only worked in the summer time.

Personally I feel that the term 'butterfly' is a corollary of 'butterboy'. Although our term 'Butterboy' refers to a newcomer to the trade, for an unspecified term, as butterflies only live for a few short weeks then perhaps we should revert to the original? Anyway that knocks on the head our present understanding of how the term butterboy came about (a) because some drivers worked for the Yellow Cab Company in Tooley Street, or (b) from the elder drivers using the cab shelters telling a much younger driver to "shut up, your none but a boy!"

The question has often been asked who authorised the 'knowledge' and when did it start? We know now that it started in 1884 but as to whose authority remains unexplained. The nearest clue came from Mr Edward Ware,

Butterflies

ex Superintendent at the Public Carriage Office between 1864 and 1895. During the 1895 Departmental Committee of Enquiry, appointed by the Home Secretary Mr H.H.Asquith, Mr Ware was asked: "By whose authority was the Knowledge of London introduced?"

His reply was enigmatic in the extreme. Quoting from section six of the 1869 Metropolitan Carriage Act, he said: "Any license in respect to hackney or stage carriages (buses) under this section may be granted at a price, on such conditions, be in such form, be subject to revision or suspension in such events, and generally be dealt with in, such manner as the said Home Secretary may by order prescribe."

He went on to say: "The Secretary of State has the power under that section to impose any condition he thinks fit on the granting of a license, with the exception of fares and the distances involved." If the Home Secretary in 1884, Sir William Vernon Harcourt, made such a condition regarding the 'knowledge' I have been unable to find it. During my research on this subject I have checked orders made by Home Secretaries from 1869 to the present, The London Gazette, The Times newspaper, all Mepo files at the Public record Office. I have corroborated many things we know about and discovered many things of which we had no idea of, but I have not discovered any official document authorising the 'Knowledge of London.'

The first mention of the 'knowledge' was in the Commissioner's Report for 1888 and it revealed that the 'knowledge' 'commenced in 1884. Proof, if further proof is needed, comes from the evidence of Superintendent Arthur Bassom of the Public Carriage Office during the 1911 Departmental Committee of Enquiry who, when asked if the knowledge test had become more severe, replied: "To my own knowledge the test has not become more severe than it was 27 years ago, with the single exception that motor cab drivers are now required to know the direct route to and from various suburbs."

Chapter Two

Knowledge advances by steps and not by leaps
Essays & Biographies. History.

We come now to a milestone in the history of the London licensed taxi industry, the advent of the motor cab. I suppose strictly speaking that the Bersey cab, introduced into London in 1897 was not a motor vehicle because it was powered by electricity. However I'll let the purists sort that out. Eighteen of these cabs were licensed in 1897, there were also 7,925 Hansom cabs, 3,583 four wheeled 'growlers' and there were 13,673 cab drivers.

To the Bersey cab goes the somewhat dubious distinction of being the first power propelled road vehicle to be involved in a fatal road accident, in a street off Mare Street, Hackney, where the Trelawney Estate lies between Paragon Road and Morning Lane. A 14 year old boy had climbed onto the rear of the cab for a free ride, unfortunately his coat caught in the exposed drive chain and he was crushed to death.

There were 1,952 applicants for the 'knowledge' in 1897, of whom 971 passed and 981 failed. The 971 men who passed the 'knowledge' were tested for their ability to drive, 64 were rejected and the remaining 907 passed; of these 26 were also tested as to their ability to drive a hackney carriage propelled by mechanical (electric) power.

It was also the first time that proprietors complained that the ''knowledge' was too hard and that cabs remained in their yards because of the lack of drivers. These complaints were to reach sizeable proportions up to the outbreak of the First World War in 1914 and to a lesser extent causes concern to proprietors in our own time as well and should, as I hope to prove, cause some concern to drivers as well.

By 1894 the time taken to do the 'knowledge' had settled down to between four and five months. It also appears, in the absence of anything to the contrary that applications could be made at any time during the year. The Commissioner's reports only give the number of applicants passing and failing on a year by year basis. In 1894 there were 1,025 applicants for the 'knowledge', 854 passed and 351 failed. Of those who passed many were examined more than once and in some cases six times.

By now the question of the 'knowledge' was being discussed on a wider basis. During the Departmental Committee of Enquiry in 1895, a considerable amount of time was taken up concerning the 'knowledge'. A key witness was a Mr John Parker, late Chief Inspector at the Public Carriage Office at Scotland Yard. He was asked a series of questions by the chairman of the enquiry, Mr George Russell MP.

In answer to a question about the kind of examination he put the applicants through, Mr Parker answered: "I would ask a man how would you go from here (Scotland Yard) to Lords Cricket Ground? Having answered that, how would you go from there to Euston Station, from Euston to Waterloo Station, from Waterloo to London Bridge Station, from London Bridge to Cannon Street, from Cannon Street to The Angel Islington, from the Angel to King's Cross from there to Russell Square, from Russell Square to Grosvenor Square and from there to Belgrave Square?".

"If the applicant answered the questions fairly satisfactory, that is if he had an idea of the way he would go from one place to another and oftentimes men have an idea but they can't explain themselves. I would then suggest names of streets which would lead them on, to see if they really did know their way. If they accepted the names I suggested, I accepted that they knew it. I would then ask them where various places were located such as the Midland Railway station, the Great Northern, the Great Eastern, the Bank of England, the Corn Exchange, Mark Lane, St Thomas's Hospital, Guy's Hospital and such like questions."

All this did not go down too well with the chairman who replied: "I should have thought that was not the way to extract his real knowledge from him." He thought it fallacious as a test of knowledge, to put leading questions and then suggest the names of streets. The applicant could be led to believe he had a knowledge which he really did not have.: "Do you think," said the chairman: "that by this irregular examination, an examination that is not following any certain topographical line, that this was a fair test of a man's knowledge." "I believe so sir," was the reply.

"Was it common form," the chairman asked, "to ask questions in the way you have described, did you ask each man the same questions?" "No", was the reply: "I began in the west with the first man and commenced in the east with the next man, otherwise the first man would go out and coach up those waiting outside, perfectly prepared to answer the questions." It did not seem to have occurred to them to give each man a completely different set of runs.

The Chairman then asked Mr Parker: "If you made a practice of asking them about certain routes, this square and that square and that square, as you seem to be in the habit of doing, would not that become common knowledge, not only on that particular morning but common knowledge?" "It would sir," was the reply, "but there was no established form of questions."

John Parker was asked if he was the only person to conduct the examinations, or was this duty shared with others: "More often than not, I must say, that when there was pressure, if, for instance, 12 or 14 men came to be examined in a morning, I had to ask another inspector to take some but it was always done in each others presence." He was asked if he thought this kind of testing was a real test of a man's Knowledge of London. "I do", he said, "It is as far as we can go; as far as an oral examination will go."

The Committee of Enquiry considered that the standard of the examination as to the applicants for the 'Knowledge of London' was sufficiently high, though most of the questions were from Scotland Yard to various destinations. But although it concluded that the examinations should be much stricter nothing much was done to make it so.

During the 1906 Committee of Enquiry their were several comments made about the ''knowledge' being too difficult. When Mr James Fairbank, a cab proprietor owning 100 cabs was asked if he thought the ''knowledge' was too difficult he replied:
"Yes, that is my opinion. I have known many instances where an applicant has lived in London all his life, yet cannot, before the police inspector, answer the questions readily enough to satisfy him. Yet, he could drive you to any part of London, perhaps he may not know the exact names of the streets off hand, but could drive you there."

Many cab drivers and proprietors were of the opinion that an applicant should be given a much easier test, which, on passing would entitle him to a provisional license for six months. Failing any adverse reports the driver should be given a full license; "After all," said Mr Fairbanks: "A month on a cab would teach a man more than three months studying a map."

At this time there were no printed runs in book form such as we are familiar with and it was not until 1911 that the first blue book was published. It contained lists of questions and public buildings and squares etc, similar to those which the applicant might be required to answer before a license could be granted. This was revealed by Superintendent Bassom of the Public Carriage Office during another enquiry in 1911.

The absence of taximeters, which were not made compulsory until March, 1907, the calculation of fares was always a hit and miss method. During the 19th century several schemes were put forward, including a gadget called a waywiser, fitted on the side of some growlers, but these and taximeters were not very satisfactory when they were fitted on horse drawn cabs.

During the first three years of licensing from June 1654 till May 1657, a fare scale of one shilling a mile was related to specific points such as: "From the Guildhall to Temple Barre or any part of Chancery Lane, Grays Inn or other place of like distance, not above 12d. From Westminster to Whitechapel or the like place or thereabouts 2/6d. From the Old Exchange to Whitechapel or the like distance or place 12d.

Though this seemed to work reasonably well.it did not prevent overcharging. On January 6th 1655, John Saltmarsh one of the original overseers of the Fellowship of Hackney Carriage drivers, was tried before the Court of Aldermen in the city for demanding more than the proper fare from the Royal Exchange to Hoxton. He was found guilty and removed from his position as an overseer.

Over charging and under charging was always a problem but the publication of the so called 'Red Book' in the late 19th century went a long way to help work out the proper fare. The official title of this book was Hackney Carriages. Distances Measured by Authority of the Commissioner of Police of the Metropolis and the Commissioner of Police of the City of London.

It measured 6"x 9" and it was 1 1/2" thick with 800 pages. It contained

1,500 starting points connecting with approximately 126,400 separate destinations with the distances measured to the nearest yard. It was the bain of a cab drivers life. Two examples are: "Aldgate High Street to Belgrave Square, 3 miles 1,609 yards and from Lower Belgrave Street to Manchester Square,1 mile 1,249 yards. Every cabman had to carry the Red Book and was required to produce it on demand from a passenger or a police officer. It also contained an abstract of hackney carriage laws.

Bearing in mind that these abstracts were mainly based on the 1869 London Cab Act, which is the major plank which governs our trade today, the Red Book stated: "A driver is not compelled to accept a fare whilst on the premises of a railway company or other private property. The next time you are at LAP and you cop a Hounslow West - try your luck!

Complaints from proprietors that cabs were left standing in their yards because of a shortage of drivers, first appeared in 1887. In that year there were 11,508 cabs licensed including 1,114 new cabs, mostly Hansoms and there were 13,673 drivers. It could be said 'that the shortfall in drivers was due to a big increase in the number of cabs.. However, from 1895 the number of cabs continued to decline and it was not until 1976 that the number of motor cabs exceeded the number of horse cabs licensed in 1897.

In 1976 there were 11,838 taxis licensed and 16,152 drivers, a ratio of 1.36 drivers per cab. In 1897 the ratio was 1.23 and by 1900 the ratio had fallen still further to 1.17. The failure rate for the knowledge was high and had been since it commenced in 1884. Where figures are given in the Commissioner of Police Reports, and their inclusion was erratic, it indicated that the failure rate was about 40 per cent.

In 1899 another reference was made to 'Butterflies' and a number of licenses were revoked but from then until the present there does not seem to have been any further reference to them. In the same year although the number of Bersey electric cabs had risen to 24, they were proving uneconomical because of their weight and they were all withdrawn from Service. A prototype Lucas electric taxi made its appearance in 1976 but it was never licensed.

The figures dealing with the 'knowledge' for seven years between 1894 & 1899 are interesting, though there were no figures for 1898 and 1899

Year	Applicants	passed	failed
1894	1,025	854	351
1895	857	610	241
1896	1,645	1,058	587
1897	1,952	971	981
1900	918	638	280
1902	1,072	837	234

The Commissioner's Report for 1896 said the high number passing the 'knowledge' tests was due to the cab strike in 1895, which lasted for three months. This was a reference to the strike in protest against the privilege railway station situation, where only certain cabs, mostly those owned by the larger cab companies who paid for the privilege for their cabs to use London's railway stations, excluding Waterloo station but including many others apart from the main line termini.

That may have been the reason but there were no strikes in 1894,1897,1902 and 1903, but the percentage pass rate in those years was higher than in 1896. The Commissioner was entitled to that opinion because he could not foresee the future and did not think of looking back to 1894 and 1895. Perhaps the high pass rate was caused by men who had failed the previous year or who had been put off by the strike and waited to pass the following year.

By 1904 the writing was on the wall for horse drawn cabs, for although the Bersey cabs had been withdrawn in 1899 the first mechanically propelled cab, a Prunel, was licensed in 1903. The number of Hansom cabs had' decreased by 78 in the same year and in 1904 a further 362 Hansoms were taken out of service. It seemed also that the Public Carriage Office were imposing a higher standard of cab, this was evident when 1,140 stop notes served on Hansom cab owners and 621 on the owners of the four wheeled Growler in 1904. These figures compared with 405 stop notes on Hansom and 521 on Growlers in 1903.

The Commissioner of Police said in his report for 1904: "The large number of rejections is due to the fact that a higher standard of fitness has been insisted upon before a license is granted. It is believed that this standard is not exceeded by any other authority which has the inspection of public carriages."

Of the 735 applications for a license in 1904 only 360 passed the 'knowledge' and 375 failed, of those who passed many were examined more than once and 51 men who passed failed the driving test. Drunkenness was becoming a problem and in the report for 1904, figures published showed that 959 drivers were convicted once, 72 twice, 37 three times and three were convicted four times.

The Commissioner also said in his report for 1904: "The decline in the number of two wheeled Hansoms and the small number of vehicles in this class, seem to show that either they are losing popularity or proprietors are awaiting developments of suitable motor carriages. This is undoubtedly the cause of the decrease in the number of horse drawn omnibuses."

In 1905 there were licenses for 12,663 horse drawn cabs and 23 mechanically propelled cabs. There were 682 applicants for the 'knowledge' 331 passed and 351 failed. Again, as in many previous years only 304 who had passed the 'knowledge' went on for the driving test and of these 32 failed. Therefore there was only a nett increase of only 272 drivers. No explanation has ever been given as to why, after passing the 'knowledge' so many men did not go forward for a driving test and of those who failed if they went on to take a second test.

Chapter Three

Knowledge by rote is no knowledge it is only a retention of what has been entrusted to the memory.

Montaigne

By 1906 the number of men applying for a cab driver's license and the number passing the knowledge had dropped considerably and had continued to do so since 1902.

Table

Year	Examined	Passed
1902	1,072	837
1903	1,039	805
1904	735	360
1905	682	331
1906	578	302

A statement was made that the 'knowledge' was too difficult and also that many men were failing the driving test which had become harder. In 1906 only 302 passed the 'knowledge' (as above), of these only 136 men passed the driving test. They were able to take the test again and they did so with the help of a 'permit' cab (see later in chapter). Without details of how the 'knowledge' was exactly carried out at this time it is difficult to come to any conclusion. Generally though the extent of the 'knowledge' and the standard of the driving test was high; as a result many failed.

Since 1902 the number of Hansom cabs had declined from 7,577 to 6,648 in 1906, but the number of growlers had increased from 3,805 in 1902 to 3,844 in 1906, plus 96 motor cabs. The Public Carriage Office thought that the decline in Hansoms was because of the increase in motor cabs, which were then all two seaters, as were the Hansoms. Whereas the continuing popularity of the growlers was due to the fact that they carried four passengers plus a considerable amount of luggage.

By the end of 1907 the Hansoms had declined quite dramatically from

6,648 in 1906 to 5,952, a reduction of 696. There was little doubt that the Hansoms were doomed and that the growlers would fare much better, though they too would not last much longer. The reason of course was the advent of the motor cab which, as long as they remained two seaters would give the growlers an extended lease of life.

In March 1907, 500 Renault motor cabs drove down the ramp of the General Cab Company Ltd's garage on the corner of Brixton Road and Camberwell New Road, to ply for hire on the streets of London. In 1908 the General Cab Company Ltd. merged with the United Cab Company Ltd. of Farm Lane, Fulham, and thus was created the London General Cab Company Ltd., one of London's great cab companies, sadly no longer with us.

The decline of horse drawn cabs resulted in a decline of 'street humour'. Drivers of London's horse cabs were famous for their wit and humour, perhaps this was a reaction to the bad conditions of their vocation. The Penny Magazine of 1900 remarked on this and told how, on one New Year's Day a cab driver was given the 1/6d legal fare. Quick as a flash came the retort, "Well, I should think you were turning over a new leaf for the New Year, studin' heconomy, hain't you".

Apparently, according to the Penny Magazine, it was the habit of horse cab drivers to exclaim "What's this then?" on being given a legal. The magazine told the following story. It concerned a gentleman, who, having completed his journey in a cab, handed a coin to the driver at which he promptly exclaimed, "What's this then?" But the gentleman objected to any argument and on the principle of "least said soonest mended" hurried away. When he arrived home he regretted he had ignored the cab driver's familiar exclamation, for he found he had paid a sovereign instead of a shilling!

The columns of 'Punch' were equally illuminating, they contained many cartoons concerning London's cab drivers, some for and some against. On 2 April 1864 a cartoon showed a growler, driven by a stout, elderly cabman, well wrapped up to keep out the cold. Having set down a toff and his lady the toff is saying to the driver, "Haw, hears sixpence-get yourself-glass-beer." Cabby replies, "Thank you sir, all the same; but I never take it. I'm a follerin' Mr Bantin's advice for corpulence, sir. He says I may take two or three glasses 0' good Claret, or a glass or two of Sherry Wine, or Red Port, or Madeiry; any sort o'spirits-" (Toff, deeply touched, makes the sixpence half a crown).

With the decline of horse drawn cabs many of the drivers changed over to motor cabs, but as they were more enclosed it was not so easy for quick repartee, especially including, you will not be surprised, between horse cab drivers and horse bus drivers and between cab drivers themselves. Most of this banter was then confined to cab shelters and other eateries frequented by taxi drivers.

Ever since the "knowledge' began it has always been claimed that it is very demanding and difficult to do. In 1908 the demand for drivers was considerable due to a huge rise in the number of motors cabs.

	Cabs licensed in 1907	Cabs licensed in 1908
Hansoms	5,953	4,826
Growlers	3,826	3,649
Motor cabs	723	2,805

First applications for a cab driver's license in 1908 were 3,142. Only 771 passed the 'knowledge' and 2,371 failed. The majority of applicants were of course new to the cab trade.

The high failure rate slowed considerably the growth of the trade, and for the first time in many years there was a growth in Jobmasters,ie, private hire, who either hired out a self drive horse and carriage or operated a hired carriage service. One of the largest Jobmasters stables was in Britain Street, Chelsea, the former stables of the Earl of Shewsbury's Noiseless Cab and Carriage Company.

If it had not been for the existing horse cab drivers changing over to become motor cab drivers, whose failure rate in the driving test was low, compared with first time applicants, the London taxi service would have been unable to give the capital the taxi service it deserved.

The cause of this of course was the "knowledge". First applications for a license in 1908 were 3,142, of these only 771 passed and 2,371 failed, though they could have of course gone on to try again. But as overlapping figures of pass rates have never been published, if indeed they were ever kept, we cannot know what eventually the numbers who passed after signing on in 1908. The Commissioner of Police said in his report for 1908, "The large number of failures in the geographical test is probably due to the fact that the advertisements of motor cab proprietors induce many men to apply who had little general 'knowledge' of the town."

We know from past experience that this is not the case. The applicants for a London cab driver's license, who have come to London from other parts of the country, are more likely to pass the ''knowledge' quicker than a native born Londoner. They will have no pre-conceived idea of London, they will not think they know it all before they start and they will be starting with an unclut-tered mind on the subject.

This was borne out by a statement in the 1911 Departmental Committee of Enquiry, set up by the Home Office. Captain Lynch, Secretary and General Manager of the British Motor Cab Company Ltd., whose garage was in Grosvenor Road, now the site of Dolphin Square, said in a statement to the committee. "We have 600 men attending our school and we cannot get them through the geography test at Scotland Yard." "Are most of them from outside - countrymen?" he was asked: "No, the greater majority of them are London men."

By 1910 the situation regarding the 'knowledge' had not improved, 2,052 men applied for a driver's license but only 598 passed, this was approximately 30 per cent. It has never been said officially but part of the problem was the poor educational standard of many of those who were seeking employment. This year saw taximeters tested for the first time and the 'knowledge' was now officially called "The Knowledge of London and its Environs."The suburbs to you and me! In 1911 there were 1,722 applicants for the 'knowledge', 927 passed, equal to 54 per cent.

It was the habit of the major cab companies to put the drivers through the driving test before they had passed the 'knowledge'. Whether this was done with the co-operation of the Public Carriage Office, or the compa-nies own test is not made clear. But, as the results of these driving tests appear in Metropolitan Police Reports, it would appear that these tests were official. The Public Carriage Office had confirmed in 1907 that they were conducting driving tests. In 1911, 6,437 men were tested as to their ability to drive, 3,695 passed and 2,472 failed.

At first sight there would appear to be some inconsistency with the figures. If there were 927 men who passed the 'knowledge' in 1911, why was it stated in the Commissioner's Report for 1911 that 6,437 men were tested as to their ability to drive and 2,472 failed? The answer may lie in a return from the Public Carriage Office of 31st December 1911, headed: "A Return Showing The Number Of Motor Cab Drivers Who Failed To Pass The Driving Test On Types Other Than They Were Licensed For During The Year Ending 31st December 1911.

The return listed 21 different types of cabs and the number failing on each type of cab. Viz.

Failed		Failed		Failed	
Argyll	3	Humber	1	Panhard	15
Austin	5	Darraq	49	Pilot	4
Ballot	10	De Dion	5	Renault	151
Humber	1	Delahaye	-	Unic	44
Belsize	38	F.I.A.T	29	Vinot	5
Brasier	4	Mors	4	W.Siddley	37
Charron	37	Napier	33	Zust	8

All these totals add up to 483 men who failed what appears to be a second test on a different cab.

There were 21 different types of motor cabs in 1911 and all of them had different controls. For example, the Renaults had a quadrant gear change and the Unics were gate change boxes. Most of the quadrant gear changes had reverse on the far right and 3rd gear was far left, next was second gear then 1st and neutral, but not all quadrant gear changes were the same.

Cabs with gate change boxes were also different, all had neutral in the position where it is today, but on the Darraq for example, 1st gear was bottom left, opposite was 3rd gear, 2nd gear over to the top right and reverse was bottom right, where it is on most cars today. Some accelerators were between the footbrake and clutch pedals, ie, central drive, on some models the footbrake was on the right and on some cabs it was on the left. On eleven models the foot and hand brake were combined. Some hand brakes were pulled and others were pushed. The result of all these different models meant that if a driver had passed his driving test on a Unic and later changed to a different model then he had to take another test. It was not all that long ago when, officially, if you passed a test on an automatic and you changed to a manual, then you were required to take another driving test.

Added confirmation comes from an edition of Taxi World of April 1929 headed "A Marvellous Butter Boy. According to information received, as the police say, he was trained by the British Legion, and has been a taxi driver less than 12 months. Yet he is reported to have passed the Scotland Yard test on no fewer than eight different types, and to have five entered on his bill in the first six weeks. A record surely!"

Another report, from Superintendent A.Bassom of the Public Carriage Office to the Assistant Commissioner 'B' at Scotland Yard on 24 January 1912 gives further proof. "The returns of failures of men already licensed for one or more types one is easily convinced that the present system is the only satisfactory one."

"It will be observed that in 1908 111 men failed on the first test, more than one fifth of those tested and 12 failed on the second test. In 1909, 339 failed on the first test, about one fourth of those tested, 80 failed the second test and one failed the third test. In 1910 there were 351 men failed on the first test, one fifth of those tested, 93 failed the second test and one failed on the third test. In 1911 there were 351 failures on the first test, again one fifth of those tested, 56 failed the second test and two failed the third test."

"To put it briefly, about one fifth of the men who wanted to drive other types of cab would have been incompetent had the system not prevailed. I submit that the figures given prove beyond the shadow of doubt that no change is possible in the present system."

It must be remembered that the Public Carriage Office had and still have, a responsibility for passenger's safety and though we may think that such procedures were archaic, the safety of passengers was paramount. The strange thing for which no one will supply an answer is, while there is this regard for public safety for taxis and every other form of public transport, successive governments since 1961 have failed the public's safety by allowing unlicensed vehicles to operate without any restrictions at all.

The 1911 Committee of Enquiry was something of a watershed for the London licensed cab trade. Appointed specifically to investigate the proprietors claim for a fare increase, it looked into every aspect of the trade. One of its conclusions concerned the 'extras'. The committee were of the opinion that it would be desirable that the extras should be conceded to the drivers as part of their remuneration, subject only to the obligation of recording them on the taximeter. The owners of course had been pressing for their right to retain the extras.

It had been the proprietors case that the topographical 'knowledge' test was too difficult and so severe that it resulted in a shortage of drivers. They asked that the 'knowledge' should be made easier.

The committee's findings were: "As regards to the topographical test the committee does not consider that it is undue or excessive. It is the same in the centre of London that has been in use for many years for horse cab drivers with an increase as to the knowledge of main roads in the outlying suburbs, due to the increased distances covered by taxi drivers. The committee believe that an adequate topographical knowledge of London is essential for the proper use of taxi cabs and in the interests of the public they cannot recommend its relaxation. The drivers also approve of the maintenance of the present test."

The 1911 Committee of Enquiry was held at a critical time for the London Cab Trade. It was preceded by six years of dramatic change, the advent of the motor cab and the implications for the horse drawn cabs is shown in the following table.

Year	Motor Cabs	Hansoms	Growlers
1906	96	6,648	3,844
1907	723	5,952	3,866
1908	2,805	4,826	3,649
1909	3,956	3,299	3,623
1910	6,397	2,003	2,721
1911	7,165	1,803	2,583

Obviously the growth in motor cabs was at the expense of the horse drawn cabs. In 1900 there were 11,252 horse cabs licensed and no motor cabs, by 1911 the number of horse drawn cabs had fallen to 4,386. The total number of cabs licensed in 1911 was 11,551, therefore from 1900 to 1911 the number of cabs in London had only increased by 299.

It became obvious during the 1911 Committee of Enquiry which, incidentally was authorised by Winston Churchill when he was Home Secretary, that the Knowledge of London had placed a severe restriction on the cab companies. They had the vehicles but could not obtain sufficient drivers, because they claimed, the 'knowledge' was too severe.

From the evidence of Captain Lynch, already referred to, he said the British Motor Cab Company has 1,000 cabs but only 548 were working. The company badly needed drivers, at least 200. He was asked by Sir Archibald Williamson MP: "Do I understand from this that you have considerable difficulty getting sufficient drivers for your cabs?" "We have the men," he replied,"But we cannot get them through the knowledge."

According to the 1911 Committee of Enquiry the 'knowledge' test was much harder than it was in the predominantly horse cab days, because taxis could go much further and questions on the suburbs had increased. It was on the geographical test that the men failed, not so much the driving test and the figures from 1905 to 1911 tend to prove it.

Knowledge				Driving Test	
Year	Applicants	Passed	Took Test	Passed	Failed
1905	682	331	331	270	61
1906	578	302	302	262	40
1907	2,144	803	803	713	90
1908	3,142	771	771	648	123
1909		No details given			
1910	2,052	598	598	522	76
1911	1,722	927	927	805	122

In 1911, even after 27 years, the 'knowledge' was still in its infancy. It became obvious why so many failed simply because there was no laid down plan like there is today, on how to go about learning the 'knowledge'. Most of the study was done poring over maps. Some of the large cab companies, such as the British Motor Cab Company did provide wagonettes to take men around but it was not carried out on an individual basis, or pairing up with someone else. There does not appear to have been call-over sessions or even totting up the points. There was no riding a cycle then to learn the 'knowledge'.

The London Correspondence School took up classes for some men but there is no record of whether this was successful and there was no Knowledge School until 1927 (see chapter six). Superintendent Bassom of the PCO told the 1911 Enquiry, "We are anxious to assist any man who really shows an aptitude to learn and appears to have a reasonable knowledge of the town, by granting him a 'permit to learn to drive a cab before he completes   his   topographical examination   but   on   the understanding that this must be passed before a license can be issued. Generally the applicant will appreciate the concession and extend his knowledge

The permit was permission to drive a cab belonging to one of the large companies, in effect, to assist the applicant to learn the 'knowledge. It was not plated and neither was a taxi meter fitted. This would bear out the fact that there was no method of riding a bicycle , or even to walk the runs. The Enquiry did reveal that an applicant who failed on his first appearance, could go on to make six or even a dozen appearances but on average those who passed fairly quickly made three or four appearances.

Another witness at the Enquiry was Mr Davidson Dalziel, a director of the London General Cab Company. He was asked: "Do you suggest that there is a shortage of drivers?" "Not with regard to the cabs I have already licensed. I have a large fleet of new cabs that I require drivers for. They have never been licensed and I could give employment to 1,000 men tomorrow, if I could get them. The problem is the tests the men have to go through. With us the principal test is the medical. We reject men who are unfit from the health point of view but when he has passed his medical with us he has to undergo a series of tests elsewhere."

"He has to pass the Knowledge of London test by the police authorities, he then comes back to us to be taught to drive the cab. Then he is subject by the police to a strict investigation of his past life. Generally speaking I must say that the selection of men who drive motor cabs in London have been carefully selected by Scotland Yard, with the result that I do not think you would find on the whole, a finer body of men in the world than they are."

"I think they are select and well picked men but the difficulties are almost insurmountable in getting round the various tests and examinations which they are obliged to pass and that is what is keeping us back."

A SUMMARY OF THE COMMITTEE'S FINDINGS

1.   No alteration of tariff.
2.   Extras to belong to the driver.
3.   Driver's proportion of takings to be 20 per cent for the first pound and 25 per cent above £1.
4.   Owners to supply the drivers with petrol at a fixed price of 8d a gallon, independent of market variations within 20 per cent. of present bond price up or down.
5   No limitation of cabs or drivers
6.   A special license for distant suburbs.
7.   Abolition or reduction of the £2 2s motor car tax.
8   Abolition of one of the two charges demanded of drivers for licenses.
9.   Standard of qualification for licenses to be strictly maintained.

The committee emphasised their opinion that sooner or later a change to the mileage system is required in order to procure the best results for London's taxi cabs and the conversion of the arrangements between owners and drivers to a mileage basis should be kept in view as the ultimate solution should further questions arise.

Chapter Four

Knowledge has its penalties and pains
as well as its prizes.
Bulwer-Lytton

The drivers were pleased with the outcome of the 1911 Enquiry but the seeds had been sown which would germinate in the future. The application for a fare increase had been justified for the fare had been set too low in 1907, just as the motor cab trade was taking off. Also, there were then just over 100 owner drivers, which the 1911 Enquiry had highlighted. It had also brought on the scene the question of the suburbs but the ideas expressed had to wait a very long time.

The idea for a suburban license came from the enquiry along lines that in suburban areas such as Staines, Purley, Uxbridge, Southgate, Edgware, Barnet, Epson and Chislehurst etc., which might be selected by the Commissioner of Police, a special license might be granted for cabs to work locally at one shilling a mile. The driver would be permitted to take a fare outside his own area but would not be permitted to pick up a fare outside it.

A scheme for operating in the suburbs commenced in 1935 and Ealing was chosen as the suburb to try the idea of a suburban cab service. Among the first men to take part were A.A.Baker, E.J.Clinch and J.Warner. These were green badge men who were willing to build up work in the suburbs, instead of seeking work in the crowded central area.

The Commissioner's authority for commencing these kind of areas, which apparently were not covered by the regulation for the central area came from the London Cab Order 1934 made by the Home Secretary under powers given to him by section (9) of the Metropolitan Public Carriage Act, 1869 and the London Cab and Stage Carriage Act 1907,and section (1) of the 1934 London Cab Order. Part IV section 27 (1) (b)states:-
"In any case where the licensee has not satisfied the Commissioner of Police that he has an adequate knowledge of the Metropolitan area he may attach a condition prohibiting the licensee from plying for hire with a cab in the said area except in such part or parts as may be specified, being a part or

parts in respect of which he has satisfied the Commissioner of Police that he has an adequate knowledge."

Section 1(1) of the 1907 Act gives the Secretary of State, then it was the Home Secretary, powers to to fix fares either on the basis of time or distance, or both, "so as to differ for different classes of cabs and under different circumstances." There is no evidence as far as I am aware that this section was ever used to grant a higher fare in the suburban areas.

The entire episode of the suburban areas seems to be surrounded by supposition, mystery and just a touch of legality. For example, it is almost certain that the yellow badge area with the distinctive yellow badge and legally laid down distances of licensing did not commence until 1949. The early men who were working the suburbs were nearly all men who lived in or near a particular suburb. But as the general knowledge did not it seem, extend out to these suburbs, some form of legality had to be thrown over it.

Although all these men were green badge men they had to qualify for the knowledge of Ealing but by virtue of their green badge were permitted to carry on working. Because they had to qualify for the area it would mean losing a days work attending the Public Carriage Office for the knowledge exams, Consequently it was agreed by the Commissioner that their tests regarding their knowledge of the area would take place at Ealing Police Station.

Some of the points asked , all major points you will observe, included Northolt Pony Track, Kew Gardens, the Firestone Tyre Factory, Boston Manor Station and the King Edward Memorial Hospital. They were also required to know major points in central London, which would have been no problem for them as they were all green badge men. These points included Guy's Hospital, Chelsea Football Ground, Fulham Town Hall, White's Club and the Freemason's Hall.

Initially there were 35 drivers licensed, who were prepared to work the rank in Ealing, located at Haven Green. Sometime in 1935, the date was not given, the Ealing drivers applied for an extension to their area. Strange as it may seem it was extended to include Hayes in the West, to Marylebone station in the east and from Wealdstone in the north to Richmond in the south. It soon became obvious that this area was far too large and following strong protests from the Transport and General Worker's Union's Cab Section, it was decided by the powers that be that the area would extend to a 2 1/2 mile circumference around the rank at Haven Green, which then had a telephone for incoming calls.

There had been a cab rank and a cab shelter with a telephone at Lewisham for a good many years, which surely would have counted as an inner suburb? A report in the April, 1948 edition of Cab Trade News revealed that the shelter had been sold by The Cab Shelter Fund, a charity with no cab trade representation at that time, to a local private hire company.

That was bad enough, but when it transpired that the rank telephone was installed inside the shelter and a yale lock fitted to the door, then said the item in Cab Trade News "our patience is exhausted." This was a case of the straw that broke the camel's back. Eventually through the efforts of the Union's South London Branch, the phone was eventually installed outside the shelter and all drivers using the rank had their own key.

In 1937 the Cab Section of the TGWU, put forward a resolution calling for more drivers to use the suburbs. This they believed would relieve the pressure of too many cabs chasing too few jobs in the 'magic Circle'. The proposal also called for drivers who continued to work in the central area, should contribute 6d a week (2 1/2p) to subsidise those who worked in the suburbs, This was not taken up because of the difficulty of collecting and distributing any money which may have been donated.

The official Yellow Badge system seems to have commenced in 1949 for the Commissioner's Report for 1949 stated: "The number of applications for the first time was 1,138 and the total number of appearances was 11,821, of these 507 passed the knowledge and included in these were 107 Yellow badge licenses." With few exceptions the reports have continued to record the number of yellow badge licenses until the present day.

Meanwhile, after the 1911 enquiry it was business as usual but little did the trade know of the pain they must go through and the men who were lost during the four long years of the 1914-1918 war and the years immediately following that holocaust.

In 1913, of the 676 men who applied for a cab driver's license only 366 made the grade and the Commissioner's Report stated: "An additional total of 201 men were rejected after police enquiries were made." It sounded ominous and it probably was but there was no intimation of why it had been necessary to reject 201 men. The report also stated: "The want of knowledge on the part of many of the applicants meant that there were 6,339 separate examinations."

It also appeared that many former horse cab drivers were changing over to drive motor cabs, as had been the case a few years earlier. This was only to be expected following the rapid decline of horse drawn cabs, both hansoms and Growlers. This was proved by the fact that the total number of drivers licensed in 1913 exceeded those who had passed the knowledge and added to the number of drivers who were licensed in 1912.The proportion of drivers to cabs was 1.19 in 1912 and 1.16 in 1913 it was in itself an indication that the number of drivers was insufficient.

There were no details on the cab trade in the Commissioner's Reports for 1909, 1911, 1914, 1915, 1916, and 1917, but the number of cabs, both motor and horse drawn in 1910 was 15,995. In 1913 the numbers had declined to 11,862 and by 1918 the number of cabs licensed had reached an all time low of 5.798, the lowest figure since records began.

Until 1907 the horse cab driver had always retained the extras, simply because there was no way of recording them. The installation of taximeters.authorised by the 1907 Act changed all that. It stated that all the fare must be recorded on the taxi meter, including the extras. The proprietors then claimed that the extras were theirs, to offset running costs. When the 1911 enquiry awarded the extras to the drivers the cab companies claimed that it cost them £45,000 a year.

In 1911 the price of petrol increased to 9d a gallon and a Court of Arbitration fixed it at 8d. In January 1913 the price of petrol demanded from the drivers rose to 1/1 d a gallon and the drivers immediately went on strike which lasted for three months. The men's slogan: "Why should labour be forced to pay for the action of capital" had a justified to ring about and it was taken up by The Times.

That paper's editorial of January 3rd, 1911, said, "The cab trade is at the mercy of those who fix the price of petrol, a sensible way out would be to raise the fare, which any other business would have done, passing on the increase to the consumer. But the cabs in London are the buses of the Parliamentarians who had control of the fares they paid".

As a result of the strike the Fiat Cab Company whose garage incidentally was underneath St Pancras station, the De Dion Bouton and the Universal Cab Companies never re-opened. Not long after both the National Cab Company and the Waterloo Cab Company also closed. Many more fleets went out of business during the 1914-1918 war, among them the British Motor Cab Company, who turned its premises over to war work. Thus again more seeds were sown whose crop would come years later.

The Commissioner's Report for 1917 revealed that the Metropolitan Police Area then extended to cover 700 square miles, from Colney Heath in Herts to Tadworth in Surrey, and from Larkhall in Essex to Staines in Middlesex. There was no reference to cabs in this report and the 1918 report revealed that there were only 5,978 cabs licensed, the lowest number since 1853 and there were 6,189 drivers. The Knowledge of London was discontinued during the war.

In 1919 there were 9,399 licensed cab drivers. To avoid delay the issue of licenses to men who had been demobbed from the services, the regulations were waived until the crush ceased. There was a shortage of cabs and the Commissioner said: "New cabs have passed the inspection and now await delivery from the manufacturers, it is understood that large numbers have been ordered. This was a reference to the MK 1 Beardmore.

The Commissioner also made a statement that could just as easily be made today. "there is no doubt," the report stated: "that congestion of traffic is, to a very great extent, due to existing thoroughfares being out of date and unadapted to either the volume or the nature of the present traffic conditions. Another factor is the length of time taken to carry out repairs to streets and roads - no attempt being made to work at night, with the result that traffic becomes hopelessly congested in main thoroughfares for a period which would probably be very considerably curtailed if more up-to-date ideas prevailed." The main thoroughfares the Commissioner referred to in 1919, are exactly the same thoroughfares we have now. The decision to license women in 1919 is the subject of the next chapter.

Chapter Five

Sigh no more ladies, sigh no more. Men were deceivers ever.
William Shakespeare

The short statement in the Commissioner's Report for 1919 that four women had been licensed to drive taxis in London did not mean that women had never before been licensed to drive hackney carriages in London. But it is necessary to go back over 350 years for the answer.

Every Act of Parliament concerning London's hackney carriages, from Cromwell's Ordinance of June, 1654 to the current Act of 1869, have permitted the widow to inherit her husband's hackney carriage license. The Act of 1662 contained a clause compelling the Hackney Coach Commissioners, "To keep a register of the names and dwelling places of all such persons as they shall license to keep a hackney coach, together with its mark of distinction."

The list (my copy dates from 1664) contains the names of 19 women who had inherited their deceased husband's hackney carriage license. For example; Joyce Palmer of Star Yard, off Long Acre had license number 126; Alice Graham license 171, lived in Vinegar Yard off Drury Lane and Martha Shallhead, license 218, lived in Bedfordbury. The widow Lewen, license 187, had remarried, she and her husband lived in Tothill Street, Westminster, where he kept the 'Feather's' public house.

There were 12 supernumeries listed but of those 12, only two women were listed, James Clark was licensed to drive the coach with license 187 belonging to the widow Lewen and John Kirby was licensed to drive with license 281 belonging to the widow Margaret Walker. Her name appears in the list of 1662 as license number 281 of St Martin's Lane. Their former husbands had either died prior to May 1657, when Cromwell ended the Fellowship, or between 1657 and 1662 when the new legislation commenced.

The remaining 17 women licensed actually drove their coach themselves, because if they did not, and no supernumeries are listed as driving their coaches, then their license would be forfeit. The original reason was to ensure that they did not become a charge on the parish. It would seem that the object in the Act of 1869 was the same and has lasted to the present time.

The situation changed dramatically after the Act of 1694 which increased the license fee to an initial cost of £50 plus £4 per annum. The greater majority of owners could not afford the £50 premium and were forced to sell their license at the going rate of £16. Often they rented it back for £10 per annum and they could then rent out the coach to a driver, creating a three tier system of Owner, renter and driver.

In 1919, as we have seen, four women were licensed, though in fact there were four women drivers that had been licensed in 1917. From a series of papers in the Public Record Office , some of which have only recently been de-classified, several unusual events have been uncovered.

Various questions were asked in Parliament, from March 1915 onwards, pressing for the licensing of women taxi drivers to replace men but the Home Secretary refused, until February 1917, when, after pressure from the Army Council and the War Committee, it was announced that qualified women would be licensed.

It was later stated by the Home secretary that this was a wartime measure and he would make no pledge as to post war action. The immediate result was agitation by the London and provincial Union of Licensed Vehicle Workers, the former London Cab Driver's Union and who in 1922 were responsible for the formation of the Transport and General Workers Union. The union sent out ballot papers to its members as to the desirability of an immediate strike on the first appearance of a woman driver.

The official papers say that the first woman to be licensed in the Metropolitan Police Area was licensed in August, 1917, but the official papers do not show whether she was ever given a cab. It was thought, according to the official report that it was not anticipated that the British Motor Cab Company, the only company likely to employ her, would precipitate trouble doing so. This statement was strange because by then the British Motor Cab Co., had ceased trading as a cab company and their premises had been converted to war work.

Another file in the Public Record Office revealed that a Miss Denning, badge number 2380 was licensed from May 1917 to May 1920; a Miss Ryder, badge 1366, was licensed from August 1917 to October, 1920;

and that a Miss Bowen, badge 662 was also licensed from August 1917 to August 1920 and a Miss Perry badge 748 was licensed from November 1917 to November 1920. Either Miss Ryder or Miss Bowen were the woman described above who could have worked for the British Motor Cab Co.

Miss Perry was also licensed from 28 November, 1922 six days after her previous license had expired and she was still licensed in 1923. All these women were proprietors and drove their own cabs. Some time later, the date was not given, it was stated by Inspector Claro of the Public Carriage Office that Miss Perry, who is still licensed as a driver, no longer held a proprietors license.

On 25 October, 1923 a letter from the Central Bureau for the Employment of Women, whose office was at 34 Russell Square, WC1., was sent to the Public Carriage Office. Its contents were not divulged but we can hazard a guess in view of the reply to the letter, that it concerned the situation with regard to women drivers.

Following its receipt a memo was sent to the Commissioner of Police, dated 31 October, 1923, it stated: "The FP being to unwieldy to handle, Mr Pullen has made a historical memo on the subject. As regard the sentence underlined in red, we have borrowed the HO file and find that what the Secretary of State said to a deputation, is so nebulous that it is useless as a peg to hang a decision on.

The memo 2b shows that four women were actually licensed as taxi drivers and over a hundred applied and 12 got as far as attempting the topographical exam. The awkward point is that one of the women (a reference to Miss Perry) still holds a license a fact of which I was not aware. Her license is current to the 28th November.

I suggest that we write to H.O. to decide the principal, but give a strong lead against the licensing of women; and also send an interim reply to lA (the Women's Employment Bureau) saying the subject is before the S of S and his decision will be notified as soon as it is made."

This memo was only initialled.

A reply to the Central Bureau for the Employment of Women, dated 3rd November 1923 read:

Madam,

In reply to your letter of 25th October, respecting the conditions of employment of women, as licensed cab drivers, I am directed by the Commissioner of Police of the Metropolis to refer you to the Secretary of State for the Home Department, Home Office, Whitehall, SW1.

I am madam, Your obedient servant,
S Mylins,
For Secretary.

There then commenced a fairly wide discussion at the Home Office, the Public Carriage Office and Scotland Yard, the sole reason of which, was to find a suitable reply to the Women's Employment Bureau.

Superintendent Bassom, of the Public Carriage Office made the comment: "During the war not withstanding the need for men for military duties, the union took the substitution scheme badly and it is certain now, whilst there is so much unemployment that the intrusion of women will be more deeply resented. It seems that if the door is opened to women as cab drivers, the demand for an extension to 'bus and tram' will follow, against which it is possible the whole forces of the Transport Workers will be arrayed."
A. Bassom,
Superintendent

Another memo, dated 3 December 1923 but with no details of which department it came from or to whom it was sent stated:"Four essential statements were forthcoming from the Home Office. They had to consider whether this subject was affected by the Sex Disqualification Act of 1919, which provided that a women shall not be disqualified from "Entering or assuming or carrying on any civil profession or vocation. Whether, as the licensing authority the Commissioner had complete discretion in this matter."

"It might be difficult to argue that driving a taxi was not a civil profession or vocation within the meaning of the 1919 Act and therefore that a woman cannot be disqualified by her sex from that occupation. But they had to take note of the fact that the Secretary of State had said: "No one has said that a woman is not physically fit to drive a taxicab."

"They also have to consider the men, by whom the wartime concession was strongly resented and would most certainly have opposed any permanent concession. It was clearly only an exceptional measure which cannot be treated as a precedent. Therefore it seems very desirable that women should not be licensed."

(Sgd.) E.W.E.H.

Another unnamed contributor to the above statement said: "It appears that the Sex Disqualification Removal Act has exactly inverted the question which has to be answered. Before 1919 the question was whether there was any justification for admitting women to drive cabs; now it is whether there is anything which would justify refusing a license."

(Sgd) A.J.E.
4.12.23.

Finally a few lines at the end which makes it almost certain that these memos came from the Home Office stated: "It appears to me that the SDR Act has settled this question and that the Commissioner cannot refuse to license women on the grounds of sex."

(Sgd)E.B.
4.12.23.

On 28 November, 1923 a memo was sent to the Commissioner from the Public Carriage Office, it was signed AB, which must have been Arthur Bassom, the chief Superintendent. It stated: "The last surviving woman taxi driver, Miss Perry called recently at the PCO and Inspector Claro by tactful handling induced her to say that she would not apply for renewal of her license, which expires today. This makes the situation less complicated."

(Sgd) AB 28.11.23.

All that now remained to be done was the reply to the letter from the Central Burcau for the Employment of Women, this was effected on 30 November, 1923.

"Central Bureau for the Employment of Women, 24 Russell Square, London, WC1.

Madam,

Four women were licensed to drive motor cabs during the war, but it is believed that they made little use of their licenses. No women are licensed now. It will be remembered that the unions raised considerable objection then to women being licensed. Now, when there are 13 drivers for every 10 cabs, there is no need to license women and their intrusion would be bitterly opposed.

The licensing of women to drive taxi cabs in London was a war time measure based on the shortage of man power. It is not proposed to revert to it in normal circumstances.

Signed,
Commissioner of Police."

The Home Office were keen to have the last word and when the file was returned to the Commissioner, a note saying: "Since the Sex disqualification (Removal) Act 1919, the Commissioner cannot refuse to license women on the grounds of sex." Across this the Commissioner wrote, "Seen." But that was not the end of the matter.

A similar situation came up again in December 1942 when Noel Baker, the Home Secretary, in a reply to letter from W.F.Higgs MP, said on 4th December, 1942, "I have come to the conclusion that it would be better not to disturb the men and to leave suitable women who are available, to take up equally important war work." This letter we can be sure was in reply to a question from Mr Higgs MP, regarding women taxi drivers.

A few days later in the house Mr Higgs asked Noel Baker if he had taken into consideration the transferring of taxi drivers to drive buses and replacing taxi drivers with women. The reply, if any, was not recorded.

The Home Secretary had a nine month start on Mr Higgs MP, for the Public Carriage Office had been asked on the 11 March 1942 if women could be licensed as taxi drivers. This was referred to the Assistant Commissioner 'B' at Scotland Yard.

His memo to the Public Carriage Office dated 28 March 1942 stated: "She may (a reference to an unnamed woman) be dissuaded from going on with it and she should be discouraged as much as possible from applying for a license. If she insists she could be held up for a long time in the Knowledge of London examinations, but if she still persists she should be allowed to continue."

Another four years were to elapse before the question of women drivers cropped up again. In January 1946, a Miss Holloway of 'Whyteleafe',Bledlow Ridge, High Wycombe, Bucks, and Mrs Dorothy Forster of 268 Longfellow Road, Worcester Park, Surrey, applied for a taxi driver's license. The Assistant Commissioner 'B' in a memo to the Public Carriage Office on 28 February, 1946, said: "It is clear that there is no legal bar to licensing Miss Holloway and Mrs Forster but everything must be done to dissuade these applicants from proceeding."

How many cobblestoned one way streets between Houndsditch and Skinners Hall, Dowgate?

The Commissioner's memo also stated: "The reasons given are, that women would not be able to handle heavy luggage and could be subject to assault. However, approval has been given for a cab driver's widow to proceed," though the memo said: "It seems unlikely that she will ever get a license."

Subsequently, Mrs Forster was told by letter; "If you wish to make a formal application for a license, it will receive careful consideration. Whereas, the official records say that Miss Holloway was strongly dissuaded from applying for a license on 13 February 1946 and she said that she would "commence a private hire service on the same lines."

Other women who applied for licenses were:

Mrs R.S.Cooper. No address given.
Mrs I Pearce, 8 Ruxley Lane, Kingston Road, Ewell, Surrey.
Mrs K.Galbraith, 26 Lakehouse Road, Wanstead.
Mrs M.G.Wallis. No address given.

It would appear that nobody made any comparison with women who worked extremely hard during both world wars, in all branches of the three services. They worked in factories building planes, tanks, guns, shells and almost anything to do with the war effort- yet, after the wars they were illegally denied the right to drive a taxi.

The disturbing fact arising from this chapter is to what extent authority went, to embargo these events, keeping the facts from the public domain. The File in the Public Record Office dealing with these events was embargoed until 31 December 1997. Other files are still embargoed and I feel certain that the events surrounding the minicab scandal of 1961 are included in those embargoed files.

Chapter Six

Knowledge is application, perseverance and
a sustained effort to learn.
Anon

With the brief statement in the Commissioner's Report for 1919, that "The decision to grant licenses to women led to only four being licensed," the question of women drivers never appeared again in any of the Commissioner's Reports up to 1991 and it has not been possible to locate any reports from then to the present:

In 1923 Superintendent Bassom was awarded the OBE and the Lost Property Office was to be staffed by ex-servicemen. The police they replaced were to be transferred to the Public Carriage Office as soon as vacancies arose. Only 301 applicants passed the 'knowledge' and altogether there were 8,154 examinations. A proportion, not stated, passed on subsequent tests. The number of first time applicants was not given between 1923 and 1945, except for the years 1933 and 1938 but at this time the 'knowledge' was taking, on average, about six months to do. One thing was very obvious, the total number of appearances rose dramatically between 1926 and 1932.

Table

Year	Applicants passed	Appearances
1926	474	9,481
1927	305	7,503
1929*	491	13,701
1930	540	18,365
1931	468	21,121
1932	588	18,346

*No report found for 1928

No explanation was ever given for the sudden increase of appearances from

1929 to 1932. The next full set of figures available was 1938 when there were 1,076 applicants, of which only 374 passed, 702 failed and there were only 9,268 appearances, though probably a good many went on to pass later.

There had been no change in the 'knowledge' requirement but the method of learning had improved considerably. Mostly this was due to the fact that cycles were now used and it had become quite common to walk the city of London. This had been a problem in the early days of the motor cab and though one or two of the larger cab companies had tried to improve the method of learning it was not until 1927 that the real breakthrough occurred.

In 1927 the first Taxi Driver's Training School was opened by the British Legion, at premises in Bishops Bridge Road, at the rear of Paddington Station. A pilot scheme for training unemployed ex-servicemen, it commenced business on 21st November 1927. Some 62 men began the course which included in depth instruction in driving, theoretical and practical education concerning the Topography of London.

Although the scheme had been thoroughly considered by the Legion's Metropolitan Council, there was no intention of increasing the number of taxis on the streets by sending men out on vehicles they would have to acquire on hire purchase. An undertaking had been obtained from the London General Cab Company Ltd., then one of London's largest taxi companies, that every man who completed the 'knowledge' and was granted a license by the Public Carriage Office, would find a job waiting for him.

It was estimated that an intelligent man would go through the course in from 10 to 14 weeks, later this proved to be unsustainable. The trainees were drawn from all parts of the London area, from places as far apart as Eltham and Twickenham and from Woodford to Bexleyheath. The cost was expected to be between £25 to £30 a man.

Major Cheeseman, the Legion's organising secretary said: "The expenses would be met out of the Legion's unemployment funds, including the cost of maintaining the men while they were training. On 2nd December, 1927, The Times reported: "There are now 68 ex-servicemen at the Paddington Centre of the Metropolitan Area Council of the British Legion and a large number of men are awaiting vacancies." One of these was Mr Frank Warren, father of the author.

The pilot scheme which started in 1927 was not as successful as had been anticipated and General Sir Edward Bethune, as chairman of the Legion's Metropolitan Area, commenced in 1928 to formulate proposals for the management of the second scheme. They were approved by the Legion's National HQ and the Benevolent Committee and it was launched in the new premises at 175 Camberwell Grove, SE5, in April 1929. This was only a temporary move and the school moved again on 15 August 1930, to 161 Vauxhall Bridge Road.

The pilot scheme had at least proved as being the only kind of scheme guaranteeing a job on completion of training. It had the additional advantage of having no official age limit, thus there was ample scope to deal with men who had served in the 1914-1918 war, who were then getting on in years.

The revised scheme set out to train 200 men on the 'knowledge' in 12 months at a cost to the Legion's funds of £7,000. It correctly estimated that it would take 26 weeks, on average, for the men to be licensed. It was found from the school's minutes that the first men to obtain their licenses took 20 weeks and the estimate of 26 weeks was revised down to 24 weeks. Even with this good record there were still a good many trainees who took much longer. A report on 30 December 1931 revealed that 19 trainees had taken 66 weeks, 31 took 28 weeks, 33 took 18 weeks, while 27 had only taken 12 weeks.

Notable contributions to the school came from private individuals. Two who must be mentioned were Viscount Wakefield of Hythe, who generously donated a new cab at £400 and also paid for its running costs. Another benefactor was Mr.S.A.Roebuck who later donated a Beardmore taxi. These vehicles were used for driving instruction prior to the men taking their driving test at the Public Carriage Office. They were fitted out at the donors expense with a seat next to the driver.

The school made no restriction whatsoever as to the class of ex-servicemen accepted, though preference was always given to men who had served in the war. The school was found to be particularly valuable in dealing with cases of unskilled labour. If a man was eager to find work and able to ride a cycle he had an excellent chance of passing through the school.

Although primarily a London scheme, the Taxi School Committee was prepared to consider applications submitted by branches outside the Metropolitan Police District, though the men concerned had to live in London throughout the period of training. Men came from all parts of the country, in addition to trainees from Australia, Canada, Ceylon and the United States of America etc.

Under the systematic course of instruction these trainees appeared to have suffered no great handicap compared with a native born Londoner. In one case the schools minutes recorded that a man from Swansea passed the 'knowledge' in six weeks. On the other hand a man from the Rhondda Valley required a year to finish successfully.

The school's minutes of a meeting in 1933 revealed that the British Legion School also provided cycles when necessary and in January 1933, it entered into an agreement with Mr H.Edwardes, of 27 Camberwell New Road, as the school's official repairer of cycles and also agreed to purchase ten fully reconditioned ex Post Office cycles at 19 shillings each, specially adapted for the work of the school.

In 1934 there had arisen opposition to the British Legion's Taxi Driver's Training School, mostly from the Transport and General Worker's Union and Mr Sutherland, who was then secretary of the school, was invited to attend a meeting of the Union's South London Branch in July 1934. The Union's case was that there were already too many drivers. Mr Condon, who was the branch chairman said: "I am in sympathy with unemployed and not antagonistic to the British Legion, but I appeal to all concerned not to overburden the cab trade with drivers and so reduce the meagre standard of living of those already in it."

Mr Sutherland then referred to the Taxi School branch of the Union and the editorial comment which followed the publication of two of the branch resolutions in Cab Trade News. This comment asked the branch to consider: "Whether the time has not now arrived when we have absorbed more men than the trade can reasonably support and that they use their influence in the interests of all drivers to secure the closing down of the British Legion's taxi school."

This was discussed by the School's branch of the Union, said Mr Sutherland, and, although all the men present were taxi drivers, not one voice was raised calling for the school's closure. In fact, a resolution calling for the continuance of the school was moved, seconded and passed by members of the T&GWU.

It is not generally recognised the other services the British Legion gave to the London cab trade as a whole. In 1938 it successfully pressed for an amendment to the National Health and Pensions Act to bring in owner drivers. Also in 1938, Sir John Smedley Crooke MP, was instrumental in having a similar alteration included in the Workmen's Compensation Act, 1938.

The move of the school from Bishops Bridge Road to 161 Vauxhall Bridge Road in August 1930, was a temporary move and on 31 October that year it moved to Napier Hall, Hide Place, near Vincent Square. Here it remained until 16th September, 1939,when the school closed down for the duration of the war. The number of men who passed out as cab drivers in 1939, up to 16 September was 61, some 25 less than the previous year.

After the war many changes lay ahead, new premises for the school were necessary and also new staff were required. This was resolved by the appointment of Inspector H.Turner, formerly of the Public Carriage Office, as Superintendent, at a salary of £400 per annum. It was also decided to take up the offer of the Drill Hall in Rochester Row as new premises for the re-established school on a monthly tenancy of £150, to include heating and lighting, plus £100 for cleaning.

On 25 November 1945, the committee resolved that as the school was up and running, fully organised and waiting to function that 25 candidates should now be selected from the 45 who had applied. By August 1946, 14 men had passed the 'Knowledge' since December 1945 and the total of men under training was 67. By August 1947 there were 109 men under training and on the last recorded committee meeting minutes of June 1947, 22 men had been granted licenses.

The last committee meeting minutes in the possession of the Royal British Legion, recorded that on March 16, 1948, Mr Alec Lardent an ex RAF man who had been appointed as a 'knowledge' instructor in January 1948, at an annual salary of £350, was carrying out the duties of instructor satisfactorily.There are many men still licensed, including myself, who remember Alec Lardent with some affection.

It has not been possible to trace the date when the school moved from Rochester Row to Harleyford Street, Kennington Oval, though it was probably in the early 1950s. It moved to premises in the London General Cab Company's premises in Brixton Road in 1964. With expiry of the lease in 1992 the school moved to Chester House, still within the Brixton Estate complex. It was officially opened by Steve Norris MP, and Minister of Transport, on 18 May, 1993.

A double for the school was Marie White who became the first lady taxi driver of modern times and only the fifth woman to be licensed since 1917. In 1978, Mr R.W.Donovan became the 5,000th trainee to gain his license through the school. The event was marked by the personal attendance of the then Home Secretary, The Rt.Hon. Merlyn Rees who presented Mr Donovan with his license.

When the Legion's taxi drivers training school finally closed in 1994, 5,500 trainees had passed through the tough training required, to become a London licensed taxi driver. In the years leading up to the school's closure, students sponsored by government schemes, (lately those on Training and Enterprise Courses TECs) and private individuals had also been catered for. This had provided a small income, but the overall cost per student was high and the lack of ex-service men and women applying for training and a reduction in the number of TEC students, meant that the financial viability of the school was in doubt. Therefore consideration had to be given as to how future training could be funded.

Under charity law the Legion was not permitted to assist more of the general public, than those it was specifically set up to help, therefore the Training School had to maintain a higher proportion of ex-service trainees to those who had not served in the armed forces. This meant that it was restricted to those who were not ex-service, unlike a similar commercial organisation.

The Legion's National Council decided that the Legion should move from direct involvement in training taxi drivers, to granting financial assistance through a sponsorship scheme. It was eventually decided that the Knowledge Point School, while not requiring the Legion's School premises, offered a good scheme and was highly recommended by the current Superintendent of the Legion's 'Training School.'

From this time ex-service personnel who proved they had the ability and the commitment were offered a training grant, providing a maximum of nine months training with the Knowledge Point School. It is unlikely that an ex-service student would remain in the school throughout, since Knowledge Point are a training provider for the North London Training and Enterprise Council and once an ex-service student has achieved the accepted standard they are transferred to the government funded Taxi Driver Training for Work Scheme, which currently lasts for a year, and the Legion Training Grant will cease.

It was also the wish of the Legion's National Council that the good name of the Training School, built up over the years, should be preserved. Therefore the Knowledge Point School has become a Royal British Legion accredited training provider.

All publicity and advertising ensures that the Training Grant scheme is known to be funded by the Legion. The scheme is administered directly by the Legion's Resettlement Support Officer and began on 1 October1994, with the transfer of existing ex-service trainees to the new scheme.

Training for the 'knowledge' continued at the Legion's school in Chester House, Brixton Road,until 1st January 1995, when the remaining students were transferred to the Knowledge Point School. Thus ended almost 70 years of direct involvement with London's licensed taxi trade. Although it is impossible to say how many, there are probably several thousand of London's licensed taxi drivers today (1999) who passed through the British Legion's Knowledge Training School.

Chapter Seven

It's them as takes advantage that get advantage in this world.
George Elliot

As a subject of its own, the 'knowledge' only rated as a statistic in the greater majority of the Commissioner's Reports. Because of this it is difficult to imagine to what extent the Assistant Commissioner 'B' and the Public Carriage Office viewed the subject. Despite the scarcity in some of the Commissioner's Reports and even a total absence of information in some of them, it is still possible to see how the 'knowledge' influenced the progress of the London cab trade.

There were other factors, some led by the Public Carriage Office, others by governments of the day which combined eventually to make the trade ripe for exploitation by Michael Gotla's minicab scandal in 1961. While it is true that neither Scotland Yard or the Public Carriage Office could foretell the future, they had, as the years passed all the facts to provide them with the knowledge that all was not well. The simple fact is, it never entered the mind of anyone with authority to collate and examine the mine of information they were sitting on. Had this been the case then much of what has happened since 1945, which has been harmful to the London cab trade, might never have occurred.

In 1924 there were 8,323 cabs and 5,093 buses. By 1933 the number of cabs had fallen to 8,025, a decrease of 298 cabs but an increase of 782 buses. Much of the decrease in the number of cabs can be explained by the years of depression which had begun to bite by the early 1920s. Several large cab companies went bankrupt, such as Friary & Johnston of Lansdowne Way, Stockwell.

Despite the fact that times were hard and the number of cabs had fallen there were still many men who were starting the 'knowledge'. From 1923 to 1946 no figures were given of those applying for a license, though for a number of years the number of men newly licensed and the number of examinations were given thus:

Table

Year	Passed	Number of Exams
1923	301	8,154
1924	355	NG*
1925	737	10,195
1926	474	9,481
1927	305	7,503
1928	No report found	
1929	491	13.701
1930	540	18,365
1931	468	21,121
1932	588	NG
1933	434	NG

*No figures recorded.

The 'knowledge' failure rate was high, especially so when the 'knowledge' was taking on average 26 weeks to complete. For the eleven years listed above, 4,693 men passed out as taxi drivers and there were 93,213 recorded examinations. On average that would be approximately 20 weeks per person. But it is reasonable to suggest that the number of weeks it was taking fluctuated between 20 to 26 weeks, similar to the figures which had been minuted by the British Legion's school's figures.

In 1931 the Commissioner of Police blamed the lack of 'knowledge' for the high number of failures. His report for that year showed that there werc 21,121 separate exams, an increase over the previous year of nearly 3,000, with 72 fewer passing. What these reports never revealed was exactly how many appearances each applicant made,or, of those who failed, how many went on to pass the following year and also the number of applicants who made appearances but were never licensed because they had dropped out.

I think we can take the British Legion's figures as being very accurate because they kept records on each person which showed that up to middle of the 1930s the average time taken to do the 'knowledge' was six months. The

Commissioner's report for 1933 said: "A new procedure for conducting the 'knowledge' came into effect in 1932." But no details were given. It later transpired that the weekly attendances became fortnightly and in 1937 the period was extended to monthly appearances: "In order that applicants will have more time to acquire the necessary knowledge."

1933 heralded years of change but not for the cab trade! One important change at the Public Carriage Office occurred when a huge chunk of its work ended with the passing of the London Passenger Transport Act. The licensing of buses , and later the trams came under the Metropolitan Police in 1869. In June 1933 there were 10,433 vehicles licensed by the Metropolitan Police, 5,767 buses, 1,990 coaches (Green Line), 2,570 trams and 108 trolley buses. Also, but not included in the changeover were 8,025 taxis

Although the licensing of bus drivers and conductors still remained the responsibility of the Public Carriage Office,the management of those vehicles listed above now rested with the London Passenger Transport Board. One of the consequences of this transfer meant that the staff at the Public Carriage Office was reduced by 37 men. At the same time the opportunity was taken of substituting 19 civilians of the Department Clerical Assistant Class, for certain police officers.

The cab trade in London suffered two tremendous blows in 1933, the cruising cab regulations and the culling of older cabs. The cruising cab regulations were dealt with in my History of the London Cab Trade and it is not proposed to deal with it in depth here, except to say that they were designed to inhibit the growth and viability of the cab trade in favour of the buses and other types of heavy road transport.

These regulations were drawn up by the London and Home Counties Traffic Advisory Committee, whose chairman was Lord Ashfield. He was also chairman of the London General Omnibus Company. Mr. F. Picks, also from the London General Omnibus Company, Sir H. Walker. Railways, Mr. W.F. Mallender The Association of Omnibus Proprietors and Mr. J.H.Turner, The London Haulage and Cartage Association.

Later Lord Ashfield became Chairman of the London Passenger Transport Board, and Mr.F.Picks also joined that Board. Nothing further was heard of Mr Mallender after the private omnibus companies were bought out when they and the London General Omnibus Company were nation-alised and became the London Passenger Transport Board.

The second blow also came in 1933 when all cabs which had been in service for 15 years or more, were required to be presented at the Public Carriage Office at 109 Lambeth Road. If the cab failed this special examina-tion the owner was made aware of the problems before he spent a lot of money on an overhaul and renovations. The following year the age level was lowered to include cabs ten years old or over. So savage was this pro-gramme that by June 1939 the number of cabs had been reduced from 8,025 in 1933 to 6,691 in June 1939 as shown below: -

Table

Year	Age of cab	Number failed
1933	15 years plus	557
1934	10 years plus	508
1935	10 years plus	783
1936	10 years plus	579
1937	10 years plus	554
1938	10 years plus	402
1939	10 years plus	446

The total number of cabs scrapped was 3,829. This drop was lessened by the licensing of 2,339 new cabs during the same period, nevertheless there was a net loss of 1,490 cabs. There were now 6,691 cabs licensed in 1939 and 11,404 drivers, a ratio of 1.70, or put another way more than two thirds of cabs were doubled shifted

During the remaining years leading up to the outbreak of war in 1939 details of the 'knowledge' were scanty. In 1934 there were still 19 four wheeled horse drawn cabs and three hansom cabs. In 1934 The London Cab Order was made by the Home Secretary, this Order largely governed the trade up until July 2000, when it was taken over by Transport for London.

In 1935 the work at the Public Carriage Office was divided into two sections, Technical and Clerical. The former section was staffed by specially trained officers dealing with technical matters. (No, the training did not include how to use a bradawl!) The clerical section dealt with the 'knowledge',and the issuing of licenses to owners and drivers.

During the 1930s there was a great deal of criticism with regard to the length of time it was taking to do the 'knowledge'. A memo from Superintendent May, of the Public Carriage Office, on 3 March 1935, headed, "Time Taken to do The Knowledge," shows that he was not concerned with the time taken to do the 'knowledge, he was in fact, possibly for the best of reasons, putting forward a suggestion for lengthening the time it took, which then was about nine months.

His report stated: "I have given every consideration to this matter from time to time and have so far hesitated to suggest any wholesale lengthening of the period between exams, on account of the adverse criticism which may result. In certain cases candidates have failed to show promise after a long period of time and have been put back for one month instead of seven days."

"I do not apprehend any trouble from the cabmen's unions, who will welcome any action which restricts the supply of drivers. The masters may well complain about something which withholds sufficient labour to man their fleets, and at present complaints have been made by some owners. Much of this was caused by the older cabs owned by masters as drivers prefer a newer cab."

"At present every candidate only begin to answer until they have attended on a few occasions, perhaps up to 8 or 10. The system of 7 day attendances is beneficial to the men since they conquer their aversion to the atmosphere of association with the police."

"The Knowledge of London has been laid down as a requirement before a license can be granted. Currently marks are now awarded as, correct answer 2 - partly correct 1 no attempt 0. At present 12 or 13 markings of 2 or 1 out of 18 questions, with a preponderance of 2's entitle the candidate to a requisition. I propose the following scale of appearances."

"No marks or only 1   awarded   2 months
2 - 4 marks awarded   6 weeks

5 - 8 marks awarded	4 weeks
9 -12 marks awarded	2 weeks
17 or over	1 week

At present seven days are the minimum period between examinations."

"Another way of reducing the number of attendance would be to institute a fee for the examinations. I would suggest as follows. The payment would deter many who now persist in the hope that they may pass one day, without however, their making any special effort to do so. Alternatively, the charge for an original cab drivers license could be £1 or any greater sum."

His views then were very much in keeping with those who were responsible for increasing the fee for a cabdriver's license from 15p to £43 for three years, as if the price paid to complete the knowledge was not high enough. His remarks regarding a charge for what was virtually to start the knowledge, would also find favour with many people today.

Despite the depression and the other vicissitudes of the 1920s and 1930s, the remark made by Superintendent May regarding the "atmosphere of association" with the police, was more real than imaginary which gave some credence to what Superintendent May had said and which led to the following tale.

A ''knowledge boy' had attended 109 Lambeth Road for his examination, he had not done very well and as he left the room the examiner asked him to "call Mr Neal on his way out." The chap was flustered, he was thinking of where he gone wrong and forgot to call Mr. Neal. Several minutes later the examiner, cross, because Mr Neal had not appeared, went to the top of the stairs which led down to the 'dungeon' and loudly called "NEAL", whereupon all the 'knowledge boys' immediately went down on their knees!

Leaving aside the "association with the police," the Mocatra Athletic Club was in great form. On 31 December, 1930 the soccer section showed the kind of spirit which was apparent in the cab trade. A match between Mocatra and the Royal Arsenal Co-op Society team, at Tooting Town's ground was played in pouring rain. Only eight members of Mocatra's team turned up but the Co-op fielded the full eleven players. Mocatra lost 2-1 but one man. W.Penin played like two men, they reckoned that if one more team member had turned up they would have won.

The Social Secretary's report stated that the dance held at "Stanley Hall, Kentish Town, was a huge success. Don't miss the next one! - February 25th at The Horns, Kennington. A Carnival dance from 7.30pm to 2am. The Dominoes Dance Band who won the Jack Payne's cup will be in attendance."

Those were the days when Mocatra played Ecatra, the Edinburgh's taxi driver's football team. This home game was played at Queen's Park Ranger's ground on 16 May, 1931 Mocatra won 2-1. The result was broadcast by the BBC and the match was widely reported in various London and provincial papers! These matches alternated yearly between Edinburgh and London for some forty years.honours I think were about even..

A verse in The Cabman's Punch, of February, 1935, showed that there was humour even if there was not much work. The verse was headed:Oh Yeah!

Under this glorious system, a peer must be tried by a Peer, a law for the rich and a law for the poor is a saying we often hear. But why can't cabmen try cabmen, for the horrible crimes they commit, with a nice public house for the courtroom, where all the old cabbies could sit.

"I don't suppose they'll be cock hatted cock eyed will do equally well, with Black Rod, White Wand and Blue Elephant and nice drops of Scotch-who can tell. Then we'll bring the foul criminal before us; for a verdict of murder we'll press, with our hand on our heart, we'll just look the part, Oyez, Oyez and Oyez."

Bert Ellis.

The Rednecks in the trade today would be happy to know of the divisions which existed in the trade before the last war and have carried on till the present. From Taxi Weekly, August 1923 comes a nursery rhyme of disunity. If all the seas were one sea, what a great big sea it would be; and if all the tree were one tree, what a great big tree it would be.

If the ODA and the ODB the Co-op, TU and LTD, combined to fight; for you and me, in the cause of liberty, what a great big fight it would be.

Even in adversity there was still time to think of others. From an issue of the Cab Trade News, 16 July, 1934, headed:-

TAXI TRADE TREAT FOR THE KIDDIES OF THE JEWISH ORPHAN-AGE
Carysford Road, N.16.

The Editor Cab Trade News.
Dear Sir,

May I, through your valuable journal publish a list of donation received? In doing so, I wish to thank all of them for the good wishes and kind words for the success of this treat.

		£.	S.	D.
Messrs.	The Kingsland Garage	5	0	0
"	Wright, Fairbrother & Steele	2	2	0
"	The Goodman Benjamin LGE	2	2	0
"	W, Watson & Co. Ltd.	1	1	0
"	Mann & Overton Ltd	1	1	0
"	Universal Auto Ins.Co. Ltd.	13	10	6
"	Mount Pleasant Cab Company	12	10	6
"	British Taximeter Co. Ltd.	0	10	6
	Mr Hyams, Troxy Cinema		10	6
	Sam Champagne		5	0

Yours faithfully,
M.Cohen, Hon.
Org. Secretary.

That was a fairly representative cross section of the trade between 60 to 70 years ago. Not much has changed - has it? For the technically minded there were 11,428 stop notes issued in 1935, 14,000 taximeter tests, and the number of drivers licensed was 11,587, there were 8,160 cabs giving a ratio of 1.42 drivers . There were 24 horse cabs licensed and 438 men passed the 'knowledge'. In 1936 there were only 14 four wheeled 'growlers', three hansoms and 23 horse cab drivers.

The Commissioner's report for 1936 revealed that all new cabs were fitted with speedometers, hire signs were now fitted on the roof of all cabs and they now had safety glass windows. In the case of applicants who had not held an ordinary driving license before April 1934, the Metropolitan Police driving test was accepted by the Ministry of Transport, in lieu of their test. Some 461 men passed the 'knowledge'

The introduction of minicabs in 1961 was not the first incursion of unlicensed vehicles causing a problem by the growth of unlicensed cars plying for hire. These cars carried a half moon shape plate at the rear stating unbelievably "hackney carriage'. This was not legally an indication that it was licensed but that it payed a lower rate of tax as a private hire car. These kind of plates could still be seen up to the late 1950s.

They commenced, quite openly to ply for hire. They claimed that the growth of suburban taxi drivers was taking their work away. They were successful because they offered the public a chauffeur driven, good class of 'stream' line car and several of these companies carried the word 'Streamline ' in their Company name. They were upset at the growth of taxis in the suburbs, claiming that the suburbs were theirs. Taxis in the suburbs were all green badge men, the suburban licensing scheme did not commence until 1949 when the first yellow badges were issued and a knowledge of the area was necessary. Green badge men could of course still work anywhere within the Metropolitan Police Area.

They commenced quite openly to ply for hire and, not content to work in the suburbs, they begun, without it seems much restraint from the police, to obtain work in the central area. The arguments put by the Joint Trade Committee were exactly the same as those that were put about mincabs. The government appointed the Hindley Committee to look, among other things,at the problem of unlicensed private hire cars. It has taken 60 years to reach the position now, where minicabs will now become licensed private hire and the problems will really begin!

The outbreak of war in 1939 finished off the Hindley Committee but before that it had published an interim report. Part of the report stated: "The decline in business was ascribed by cab trade witnesses mainly to the competition of unlicensed private hire cars. The position was that the cab trade had lost the monopoly it had previously enjoyed, and, restricted as it was by the system of control, can do nothing to meet the competition except to press for similar restrictions to be placed on private hire cars., which in fact were doing cab work."

"If nothing were done large numbers of cabs would have to be taken off the streets and cab proprietors would change over to private hire. The cab trade feels it has a strong case in law and in the public interest , for the view that these vehicles should be subject to the same regulations as cabs." This never came to a head and petrol rationing following the outbreak of war ended the problem, not to arise again until 1961 with Welbeck Motors mini-cabs.

The 'knowledge' was suspended for the duration of the war and the procedure for issuing licenses was also suspended. A system of permits was substituted for those already licensed, which were valid for a year. There was almost a complete absence on matters concerning the cab trade in the annual Commissioner's reports and obviously nothing concerning the 'knowledge' In 1944 all licenses were extended with out renewal and it was stated that there were 7,768 drivers.

By 1945 there were a few signs of a return to normality. The number of cabs licensed was 5,321 in service and the majority of these were over 10 years old, but rejection was limited to those judged to be in a dangerous condition. The basic petrol ration was increased from 90 to 120 gallons a month and later, as more drivers were demobbed from the forces, the ration was increased to 150 gallons a month.

There were also changes in 'the Conditions of Fitness' which would assist the manufacturers who were producing a vehicle in keeping with modern times. Mainly this was a two inch reduction of the body height. When the Morris-Oxford MKI was presented at the Public Carriage Office early in 1946, the Public Carriage Office expressed the view that "the new vehicle will be expensive."

In 1946 the Commissioner's Report stated that there were now 8,377 cab drivers. This was a large increase over 1945 which was due to the large number of men being demobbed from the services. The number of licenses granted following "The Knowledge of London Examination" was higher in

1946 with 106 successful applicants compared with 51 in 1945. "This was the first time that the full phrase-"The Knowledge of London Examination" had been used officially.

There was in the Commissioner's Report for 1946 a definite feeling that things had returned to normal when the Commissioner said: "With regard to unlawful plying for hire, it tends to be prevalent at places where supply of cabs falls short of demand. A number of prosecutions have been taken by the police.

Chapter Eight

Pot Pourri

For the London cab trade the years between 1953 and 1963 saw little or no change, except the advent of minicabs in June 1961. Certainly there was no change in the 'knowledge' procedure. Men applied, stayed the course, either they passed or failed, to try again perhaps. In 1953 there was a decline in first time applications when only 356 men applied and of these only 135 were successful. Although there were 563 new cabs licensed, this was countered by the withdrawal of 560 from service.

The diesel engine was introduced in 1952 and 21 were fitted in that year rising to 295 in 1953 and by June 1955, diesel cabs counted for 53 per cent of the fleet and post war cabs made up to 83.2 per cent of all cabs. In 1956 the Commissioner's Report referred to a new cab, a reference to a prototype built by Birch Brothers of Kentish Town which proved unsuccessful. Another new prototype cab with a magnetic clutch and two pedal control had been licensed "for experimental purposes."

Though not ready for service, another 11 of these prototype cabs were licensed, all Austin FX3s fitted with automatic gearboxes. The first two FX4s were licensed for service in November 1958.

The Commissioner's Report for 1962 is a good example of what was contained in these reports, for example; there were 1,350 first time applicants for the Knowledge of London. and there were 12,380 examinations, 498 passed the 'knowledge' including 65 for the suburban license and 20 suburban drivers took the green badge all London license.

The number of newcomers to the trade was 50 per cent higher than in 1961 and the Commissioner felt that in 1963 there would be a big increase in the number of drivers. There were 10.404 drivers licensed, of these 2,919 were owner drivers and there were five fleets with more than a hundred cabs. There were 7,008 cabs licensed including 759 radio cabs. On the minus side there were 251 meter offences for which the Commissioner blamed the modern design of meters for these offences.

There were 19 cases of refusing to be hired and 14 drivers were convicted and six cases of demanding more than the proper fare. Dealing with lost property the Commissioner said that 14,526 articles were deposited of which 6,303 were restored to the owners. There were 3,749 items restored to drivers and 4,725 drivers received an award.

We turn now to an unusual event which occurred in 1965 when the incorporation of the Borough of Romford and the Urban District of Hornchurch came within the Metropolitan Police Area. This meant that the saloon car taxis, licensed by the former councils, now came under the control of the Public Carriage Office. Fate has decreed that under changes connected with the licensing of minicabs, the Metropolitan Police Area will coincide with the new Greater London Area.

This means that current yellow badge owners and drivers in areas such as Hertsmere, Epsom and Ewell Borough Council, and Spelthorne Borough Council which are currently inside the Metropolitan Police Area, will no longer come under the control of the Public Carriage Office. The dual license system is opperated in Epsom.

The taxis involved in the change in 1965 were of course all saloon cars and did not conform to the London Conditions of Fitness. This was overcome by the London Cab (Temporary Provisions) Order,1965, which permitted a concession for three years allowing these saloon cars to ply for hire until 1 March, 1968, in the area for which they were originally licensed for, and a special provision to allow these licenses to remain in force until superseded by new ones.

Subject to the demands of public safety,a very considerable latitude was shown when the saloon cars were inspected. Even so, 16 were rejected on the first examination by the PCO. At the end of the year the position was:-

	Romford	Hornchurch	Total
Full London License	7	2	9
Restricted license	54	61	115
Licenses surrendered	14	10	24

There were 153 licenses taken over on 1 April 1965 and of the 272 persons holding a driver's license, only 172 applied to be licensed by the Public Carriage Office. Of the remainder, one died, and 23 indicated their intention of allowing the licenses to lapse. One license was refused on medical grounds.

By the end of the year it was apparent that many owners were not taking advantage of the transitional period. All the indications were that there would be a considerable reduction of licensed cabs operating in the Borough of Havering. Those owners who opted to join the London trade were permitted to carry the same police license plate as those fixed to the rear of London taxis.

From 1965 until 1973 when VAT was imposed on the trade, there was nothing to stir the blood, the trade accepted a 3p surcharge instead of going for broke as a consequence we are now burdened with VAT on a new cab of £3,841. The 'knowledge' carried on without any up-heaval but the standard of cabs had dropped and this, said the Commissioner in his report for 1967, was the fault of the flat rate system

The Flat rate system did not really take off until 1968, when the London Cab Act of that year repealed the former law which had prevented cabs from being left unattended. For example, drivers could not leave a cab outside their house during the day or night. Owner drivers were required to garage their cabs on a "garage and wash" basis.

In 1967 the responsibility for testing taxi meters was taken over by the British Standards Institute at Hemel Hempstead, from the National Physical Laboratory in Pentonville Road, a service they had carried out for the past fifty years. In 1972 the Commissioner reported that there were 238 cabs running on LPG/petrol, but there were only two places in London where LPG could be obtained. This, plus the fact that power was reduced when switching from petrol to LPG was another reason why LPG did not take on.

There was a 'first' in 1974 when the Commissioner reported:"There were 1,732 first time applicants for the 'knowledge' and there were 20,968 examinations and 952 had passed, the majority of whom had applied before 1974." This I believe was the first time that the Commissioner of Police had referred to these particular facts. The Commissioner though was not happy with the fact that 64 drivers were prosecuted for refusing to be hired. This figure increased to 73 in 1976 and 79 the following year.

In May 1977, Marie White became the first woman driver in modern times to be licensed since Miss Perry in November, 1917 and who was still driving in 1923. Two more women drivers were licensed later in 1977. In December 1981 Owners were permitted to display advertisements on the lower front door panels but we had to wait until 1987 before permission was given for the use of all bodywork for advertising purposes.

When the advertisements first appeared there was a complaint from one member of the public concerning the advertising of cigarettes. Also in 1981 the Transport Act of that year permitted the Public Carriage Office to charge more for a license which had formerly cost 15p for three years, to £46 for three years and £44 for a taxi license for one year.

In 1984 there were 707 complaints from members of the public, a substantial increase. Most concerned refusing to be hired, an offense which causes our trade much criticism. Altogether 89 drivers were prosecuted and 618 warned and "given advice." The following year there were 988 complaints from the public, again mostly for refusing to be hired. This time 262 drivers were prosecuted. The complaints dropped to 926 in 1986 and 258 drivers were prosecuted.

In 1986, for the first time since 1833, taxi drivers in London were allowed the right of appeal, contained in the Transport Act of that year, against a decision by the licensing authority where it had revoked, suspended or refused to grant a license. In 1988 the Commissioner's Report only referred to cab sharing and that it had not been taken up by the public.

In 1986 six drivers appealed at Horseferry Road Magistrates Court against the revocation of their license but no details of the judgment were given. Also in 1988 the suburban knowledge was revised, raising an enthusiastic response and 570 applications were received in the first three months.

For some years past the Commissioner's Reports had contained only the barest details. The last report traced was for 1991 it stated:-

Number of cabs in service	16,529
Number of radio cabs	6,824
Wheelchair accessible cabs	5.322
New cabs	1,412
Number of drivers	20,468

Number of knowledge applicants	3,142
Total knowledge exams	19,832
Suburban drivers	292
Number of ranks	446
Number of rank spaces	2,148

The latter item does not include ranks at railway stations or Heathrow.

NB The figures for radio cabs, wheelchair accessible cabs and new cabs are not in addition to the number of cabs in service.

Below: This motorised Hansom cab was introduced in 1905 and lasted only a year. Passengers were unnnerved by the fact that they could not see the driver.

Above: The author's son Timothy, a Comcab driver.

Left:The Clarence four wheeled cab commonly referred to as 'the growler'. Whether this referred to the noise made by the wheels over the cobble stones, or the disposition of the driver is a matter for conjection.

Left: The front lobby of the Public Carriage Office about 1885. Here, men were attending for a variety of reasons. Applicant's for a licence, the knowledge exam, lost property, renewal of licences, some maybe had committed a misdemeanour

Below: An Austin 12 of 1930 seen here in 1950 with an applicant for a taxi driver's licence practising reversing a cab into a narrow opening.

Above: A 1926 Morris Six. The driver is Frank Warren, the father of Philip Warren. The photo was taken outside the family house in Lunham Road, in Upper Norwood in 1947.

Left: A 1908 Humber taxi. This model was very popular with owner drivers.

Chapter Nine

Fides Servanda Est
Faith must be kept.

In October 1947 a new generation of Austin cabs was in the making, and in that month the Austin FX3 was approved, with a sliding window next to the driver giving him extra protection. This type of window was later incorporated in the Morris-Oxford cabs. In 1947 over 80 per cent of London's cabs were over ten years old and two men were still licensed as horse cab drivers, who drove the last four wheeled 'growler' at Tadworth Station in Surrey. This, as far as horse drawn cabs were concerned was the end of a remarkable era.

Horse drawn hackney coaches were first recorded working in London in 1588, though they were not licensed until June, 1654. They had served London well but they were doomed with the advent of the motor cab in 1903. The alarm signals though must have sounded, when the Bersey electric cab was launched in London in 1897.

In 1947, 1,923 cab driver's licenses were issued, this was a considerable increase over the 269 issued in 1946. Of these 2,192 licenses, 298 were those newly licensed, the remainder were ex-servicemen, formerly London taxi drivers who had been demobbed. In 1948 there was still concern over the condition of the older cabs, with 80 per cent of the fleet over ten years old. Inspection was stepped up to include owner's premises, cab ranks and railway stations. This purge revealed 4,135 cases of unfitness.

As the new Morris and Austin cabs entered service so the drivers, including those already licensed, had to undergo a driving test on the new cabs. In 1948 some 838 passed but 135 failed, this meant they could only drive the older cabs. The number of applicants for a license, attending 'Knowledge' tests for the first time was 1,014 compared with 648 in 1947. Of these 341 were successful. It seems circumstantial that the number of new entrants in 1948 mirrored the number of new cabs, ie, 344 new cabs and 341 new drivers.

There was an improvement in the new cab influx in 1949 with 1,180 new cabs licensed, bringing the total of cabs to 6,965. This was a considerable improvement from 1947 when only 6,079 cabs were licensed. Because the new cabs had a higher horse power rating they were allowed an extra 20 gallons of petrol a month, a total of 170 gallons if the cab was doubled. There were 909 successful applicants for a license but 219 failed the driving test, though the majority would have gone on to pass later. Of the number who passed 107 were for suburban licenses. This was the first year that applicants for suburban areas were required to pass the 'knowledge' for a particular yellow badge area.

Petrol rationing ended in 1950 and during the period of nearly ten years it had been in force the Public Carriage Office had issued coupons for 86,163,589 gallons of petrol for use in London's taxis. In 1949 two London taxis had been fitted with two way radio. The first cab in the UK to be so fitted was a cab belonging to Cam-Tax of Cambridge, it was fitted by Pye Telecommunication Ltd in 1947. It was not until 1949, recorded in the Commissioner's Report for that year, that two way radio was fitted in a Morris-Oxford taxi owned by Alfred Smith of Plaistow, who worked the North Woolwich docks area. Later, he had a second cab fitted with two way radio. (See Appendices)

There was now a single driving test for all types of cab and in 1950 there were 623 driving tests and 164 failed. The number of first time applicants for a license was 1,220 and the total number of appearances was 13,276. Of these there were 594 successful applicants including 87 for a suburban license. Referring to the number of offences in 1950 the Commissioner listed 66 taximeter offences, mostly for stalking, plying elsewhere 46, demanding more than the proper fare 28, carrying excess passengers 24, using bad language 20 and eight drivers were summoned for failing to wear their badge.

By 1951 the double purchase tax was beginning to have a serious effect, with only 692 cabs purchased compared with 950 in 1950 and 1,180 in 1949. Incidentally, Zebra Crossings were introduced in 1951. There was a reduction of 100 owner drivers and the scrapping of the older cabs was discontinued. The number of radio cabs had increased to 180. In 1952 the fall in the number of cabs to 5,437, only a hundred more that at the end of the war also saw the number of owner drivers still falling by a further 160 to 2,406. The fall in the number of cabs and owner drivers was directly attributed to the double purchase tax and the severe hire purchase regulations. The ratio of 1.68 drivers per cab was a dangerous level as far as the trade was concerned

By 1953 the cab trade was in crisis with only 5,609 taxis licensed and 9,077 drivers, in many garages all cabs were doubled and in some cases trebled. The Runciman Committee which had been appointed to examine the London Cab Trade had been appointed that year. Only one of its proposals were ever implemented, the ending of purchase tax and the hire purchase regulations.but only for the purchase of London type taxis.

Cabs had begun to increase as a result of the recommendations of the Runciman committee's decision but by 1961, the year of the trades 'Armageddon', Welbeck Motors minicabs, there were only 6.776 cabs. What had precipitated the introduction of mini cabs?

For some years before the "swinging" London of the 1960s, there had been a tremendous growth in travel. At weekends the main line termini had queues of people waiting for cabs, the air terminals were the same, as was the West End, especially on Friday, Saturday and Sundays. For most of us who drove a cab then it was almost a license to print money.

The demand for cabs was high and there were insufficient cabs to meet the needs not only of Londoners, but also the huge number of tourists who visited London. The boat trains at Waterloo and St Pancras were packed with Americans and other nationalities who were visiting London. air travel too was beginning to grow. The British European Airways terminal was in Kensington High Street when I was first licensed, but as the number of passengers grew so the demand for new premises saw a move to a temporary site in York Road, opposite Waterloo station. It eventually moved to temporary premises in Cromwell Road where, on the same site the huge purpose built terminal was built.

All these moves were necessary because of the huge growth in travel. The only form of travel not to increase anywhere near enough to satisfy the demand was the licensed London Cab Trade.

The trade could not see that the writing was on the wall. The 'knowledge' was looked on as a barrier against a large growth in the number of cabs, for the benefit of those already licensed, whereas it had meant a retreat into the 'magic circle'. The Metropolitan Police area is approximately 600 square miles, but 90 percent of our trade works in roughly 100 square miles and has done so for many years. Is it any wonder then that an alternative form of travel should appear.?

This state of affairs is by no means entirely the fault of the trade. One is forced to come to the conclusion that others must share the blame. Why is it that in the 1930s it was taking on average six months to do the 'knowledge', and in the 1950s and 1960s the ''knowledge' was taking about a year, double that of the 1930s, now it can take three or four years, or even more. The area of London that the greater majority of the trade works in is no larger than it was in the 1930s So what has occurred to change the situation to what it is today?

During the 1930s there were five companies producing the London type cabs, Austin, Beardmore, Morris, Citroen and the Unic KF1.Between them they offered nine different models to choose from. What is the situation today? We have two manufacturers producing one model each, with either a manual or automatic gearbox. Both of these companies have a very restricted manufacturing output and both companies have sales in many other towns and cities in the UK, plus exporting abroad, which formerly was not the case.

Here we have the classic, "what came first the chicken or the egg" syndrome. Have these two companies been forced to look for sales outside London and abroad because the strictness of the 'knowledge' was keeping sales down or is the 'knowledge' restricting the growth of drivers because these companies could not supply sufficient vehicles if the 'knowledge' was shorter?

In 1961 when minicabs started the number of cabs licensed in London was 6,776, 85 less than those licensed at the outbreak of war in 1939 and 1,084 less than in 1930 at the height of the depression. It hardly seems credible that the trade had only grown by 85 vehicles during a period of 22 years. But without any doubt it was the culling of older cabs from 1933 which severely depleted the number of cabs in London, from 8.025 in 1933 to 6,691 at the outbreak of war in September 1939. The war had also taken its toll with just 5,321 taxis licensed in September 1945.

As far as the number of taxis and drivers is concerned, the London taxi trade is in a parlous state to cope with the licensing of minicabs as licensed private hire cars. Their numbers can only be controlled by the demands made upon them by the licensing authority. All the evidence points to the fact that this will be nowhere near as strict as it is for taxis, unless the Public Carriage Office do not conform to the abysmal licensing standards in many areas outside London.

The 1976 Local Government (Miscellaneous) Provisions Act made provisions for local Authorities in England and Wales (Scotland has its own 1982 Civic Government Act) power to license private hire cars. The Act was non-obligatory and it took 22 years before the act was fully adopted throughout England and Wales, excluding London of course. In many areas it has been an unmitigated disaster

Because the number of private hire cars cannot be controlled and it is very easy to get a vehicle and a driver's license, the licensed taxi trade has been swamped by thousands of private hire cars working openly as taxis without let or hindrance. This is because the greater majority of licensing authorities will not spend money on litigation but they are not averse to hyping up fees for vehicle and drivers licenses, examinations and other excuses they can find, to obtain more money.

There are some councils who do try to contain this law breaking on a massive scale, but it has become so bad that a blind eye is often turned. Liverpool for example is surrounded by other licensing districts such as Sefton and Knowsely. Sefton is 50 per cent rural yet it has more licensed private hire cars than there are taxis in Liverpool. These private hire cars work unhindered in Liverpool and the city's taxi drivers are in despair.

Exactly the same scenario occurs in Glasgow where that city is surrounded by other areas similar to Liverpool. There are 1,500 taxis in Glasgow and they are surrounded by some 3,000 private hire cars. This situation is the norm throughout the UK. While it is true that in some towns such as

Birmingham, Manchester, Leeds, Plymouth, Glasgow and Edinburgh, the licensing authorities do their best to combat the law breakers, they are simply overwhelmed by the sheer numbers of private hire cars working illegally. Quite frankly the London taxi trade would be quite justified in fearing the worst. Successive governments since 1961 failed miserably to combat mini-cabs, what faith can we possibly have that they will do any better now that they will be licensed. To be perfectly honest the government have failed to listen to the reasoned arguments of the London cab trade who have been at the sharp end since 1961, instead they have succumbed to the "Johnnie come lately's" such as The Suzy Lamplugh Trust and similar bodies of 'do good-ers'

It is when all the statistics come together that the real picture of what has happened in London is revealed as being catastrophic. It has become obvious upon analysis of the number of cabs and drivers, that the Public Carriage Office who are responsible for administering the London licensed cab trade, can only act within the area of their responsibility for the supply of drivers and vehicles. Therefore these responsibilities need redefining.

The vehicle manufacturers are limited to a manufacturing limit that can only cope with regulated numbers of men and women who wish to enter the trade. The cost of vehicles are too high for any incentive to operate throughout the whole Metropolitan Police Area. The devastating position that the London taxi trade finds itself in, is only realised when determining that since 1961 when there were 1.6 drivers per cab, that today (1999) there are only 1.2 drivers per cab. This is an effective reduction in availability of cabs working for the public of minus 25 per cent. The cab fleet in 1961 was 6,776, today it 18,500. The number of drivers in 1961 was 10,691; today there 22,252.

There would be, in any rational solution to this shortfall, two means of resolution. Either a dramatic increase of 5,500 drivers and an equally dramatic increase in the number of cabs by 4,500.

Neither of these proposals could be considered realistic within the present licensing framework. The licensing authority does not have the ability to increase the frequency of 'knowledge' examinations, hence the time taken to do the 'knowledge' has extended to a time scale of 2.5 years. As the number of applicants has increased annually from 825 in 1961, to 4,100 in

1996, with the same number of examiners, the trade is really in deep crisis. A full review of how the 'knowledge' -is conducted is a matter of urgency. A start could be made by cutting out all the snide points and concentrate on the places which taxi drivers would require to know during the course of their work.

Currently the Public Carriage Office do not make a charge for those who wish to do the 'knowledge, although that is about to change'. Meanwhile the cost of the 'knowledge' is borne by owners and drivers. The only way the rise in unavailability can be checked is for more double shifted cabs, with a higher proportion of night drivers, for it is at night that we fail our customers and the main reason for the increase of minicabs. The fleet owners have the added responsibility of investing in new cabs, which would attract more drivers to do night work.

Between them, the two manufacturers of the London type taxi produce an estimated 4,750 vehicles per annum. A breakdown of the division of sales in other parts of the UK and exports are an unknown factor. The year on year end increase in the number of cabs in London is known, as is the total of new cabs. This will become more apparent in chapter ten.

When the Disability Discrimination Act 1995 is implemented on the 1 January 2002, on a gradual basis before the full implementation in 2012, the number of wheelchair access taxis in areas outside London will inevitably increase. Other types of wheelchair access taxis sold outside London, which do not conform to the London Conditions of Fitness, will also increase. These vehicles do not have a 25 feet turning circle.

It is hardly likely that London Taxis International Ltd would have invested huge sums in the development of the TX1 if they were uncertain as to what the new specifications would be. I will be charitable and say they took an educated guess! Any discussion on how the specifications will be framed would be a waste of time because the Disabled Persons Transport Advisory Committee has not yet made its decisions public. However, should this committee decide that London must stick with our present Conditions of Fitness, yet permit the use of the cheaper conversions outside London, then a Judicial Review should be sought by the London trade.

It would not be unreasonable to assume that it would take at least ten years to produce a 25 per cent increase in London's cab fleet if the present

Conditions of Fitness are maintained. As for increasing the number of drivers then a radical overhaul of the 'knowledge' procedure is absolutely vital. What can be done to discourage the readily available finance which encourages owner drivers against fleet rental? I simply do not know.

As in the provincial market where limitation of licensed taxis created the demand for private hire and where the growing use of taximeters by private hire enables them to work as taxis, even in many places on taxi radio circuits; so London will inevitably follow. The initial objection to taximeters in private hire cars will be abandoned as radio taxi system realise diminishing supply to meet demand.

There will be a danger that eventually private hire will become radio taxis, as their supply costs are at least one third less than the mandatory wheelchair access taxi. Immediate available street hire will only remain within a three or four miles radius of central London, at the most. Label it as you will the public don't care what they are called; they just want to get home.

Chapter Ten

Fear of the future is the beginning of wisdom
Psalm (111:10)

In 1884 when the Knowledge of London commenced, there were 9,886 applicants between then and 1888. Of these, 6,579 or 67 per cent were successful. This was at a time when the 'knowledge' was learnt from maps and not by the present process which has existed from the early 1920's. The questions asked were all relevant to the kind of destinations that a cab driver is required to know during the course of his work.

If we take similar figures from nearer our own time, say from 1980 to 1984 when, during that period there were 15,447 first time applicants and of these 3,262 passed, this was a pass rate of only 21 per cent. Coming up to date with the years 1993 to 1997, first time applicants numbered 17,232 of which number 3,268 a pass rate of only 18.9 per cent.

Obviously we know that first time applicants carried on for an undefined length of time, some dropped out and some may have applied again later. But we can only use the figures from official sources and it is from those that we must draw a conclusion. That conclusion must be that there are insufficient drivers passing the 'knowledge' to halt or possibly reverse the 25 per cent drop in availability.

Next we must examine the relationship between the increase in the number of cabs each year and the corresponding increase in the number of drivers. I have chosen a ten year period from 1978 to 1987, because this is an unbroken sequence of years for which figures are available nearest to 1998.

In the ten years inclusive from 1978 to 1987, there was an increase of 2,339 drivers, an average increase per annum of 233.90.
During the same period of years there was an increase in the number of cabs from 12,453 in 1978 to 14,792 in 1987 an average yearly increase of 233.90. This I believe is too much of a coincidence to be left to pure chance.

Ratio Of Drivers To Cabs

1965 = 1.58	1969 = 1.56	1975 = 1.42	1977 = 1.32	1980 = 1.40
1983 = 1.39	1986 = 1.31	1989 = 1 31	1990 = 1.29	1998 = 1.20

If the London Cab Trade was likened to an atomic power station the signs would be flashing danger, danger, danger and the warning sirens would be sounding.

Between the years 1990 and 1993 there was a drop in the number of drivers licensed, from 20,926 to 20,483 in 1993. There appears to be no discernable reason for this drop in the number of drivers, against the previous continuous trend for drivers to increase, by an average of 413 for the three years 1987, 1988 and 1990. this represented a loss of drivers the trade could ill afford to lose. By 1998 when 22,252 drivers were licensed there had been an increase of 1,730 drivers and an average of 247 a year. This coincided with an average increase of 302 cabs a year for the last three years that figures were available, namely 1989, 1990 and 1991.

The Commissioner's Reports for 1989 to 1991 revealed that 4,820 new cabs were licensed, why then was there only an actual increase in the total number of cabs for the same three years? The answer is that an excessive number of older cabs had been taken out of service The number of new cabs licensed commenced as a regular yearly figure in the Commissioner's Report for 1975, as shown below with the total number of cabs taken out of service.

Table

Year	Total Cabs	Increase	New Cabs	Cabs finished
1975	11,260	249	1,237	988
1976	11,838	578	1,403	825
1977	12,452	614	1,632	1,018
1978	12,453	1	1,459	1,458
1979	12,267	-276	1,143	867
1980	12,385	118	1,158	1,040
1981	12,560	175	1,402	1,227

The facts above led to a dramatic fall in ratio of drivers to cabs as shown

1981	12,560 175	1402	1227
1982	12,809 249	1,404	1,155
1983	13,127 318	1,409	1,091
1984	13,574 447	1,545	1,098
1985	13,775 201	1,341	1,140
1986	14,676 901	1,652	751
1987	14,792 116	1,809	1,693
1988	NG* NG	NG	NG
1989	15,622 830	1,469	639
1990	16,190 568	1,939	1,371
1991	16,529 339	1,412	1,073

Although there was a gross gain of 23,414 new cabs from 1975 to 1991 inclusive, not counting 1988 because no figures were obtainable, the nett gain was only 5,980 because 17,434 cabs were taken out of service.

To summarise this position. there was an increase of only 5,980 cabs between 1975 and 1991, despite the entry of 23,414 new cabs during the same period. It was the culling of 17,434 older cabs which kept the number of cabs licensed so low. Either the London cab trade was unable to absorb sufficient new cabs to replace those culled, or there were insufficient drivers passing the 'knowledge', either to purchase their own cab or to work a fleet cab.

In 1975 there were 16,037 drivers licensed, by 1991 the number of drivers had risen to 20,468 an increase of 4,401 drivers. Therefore there were insufficient drivers to work an excess of 1,579 cabs left from the 5,980 cabs available between 1975 and 1991. Many of them are standing in garages waiting for drivers who perhaps will never come unless the ''knowledge' is speeded up. In 1976 there were 6,556 owner drivers they had increased by 1986 to 8,702 or 61 per cent of all drivers. Despite the absence of data since 1991 it must be obvious that owner drivers must now be in the region of 70 per cent.

What started out as a history of the 'knowledge' has, by virtue of the research involved, developed into something much more significant. I know there are those who will deride the facts uncovered and the interpretation put upon them, but facts are facts and cannot be altered, or what they convey be changed. The majority of the figures have been checked by an independent person it is only my interpretation of them which someone may wish to challenge.

Surely, I thought, the significance of all the facts I have researched from official sources must have been apparent to those who compiled them. Perhaps though it was just a job to them and they were unaware of their significance. I do not for one moment believe that it is one person's responsibility to collate these facts either at Scotland Yard or the Public Carriage Office.

However, there are too many coincidences contained here not to arouse some suspicion that there is some control of the 'knowledge' which relates to the number of people who are licensed each year to the number of taxis that are licensed and the high number of taxis which are taken out of service each year, which I find somewhat surprising. If the vehicle manufacturers cannot build sufficient vehicles to give our -trade which it desperately needs, then we must be allowed to operate a different vehicle.

At the same time steps must be taken to ensure that more people pass the 'knowledge'. It should not take longer than a year or 14 months at the most. It is essential that the system now in use must be changed so that what candidates are asked reflects the places they would need to know as a taxi driver. It will require a superhuman effort from everybody connected in one capacity or another with the London taxi trade to get this mess sorted out.

Chapter Eleven

THE FUTURE COULD BE GOOD
"You can never plan the future from the past. "
A letter from a noble Lord" 1796.

On the 3rd July 2000, under the provisions of the Greater London Authority Act 1999, the responsibility for licensing London's taxis and taxi drivers, appointing cab ranks, the future licensing of private hire operators, drivers and vehicles was transferred to Transport for London -TfL. The same day at a meeting of the TfL the Board exercised its powers under Schedule 10, paragraph 7(1) of the Greater London Authority Act 1999, to put in place arrangements for the following functions to be discharged on its behalf by the head of the Public Carriage Office.

These were:-

1.   The grant or refusal of individual taxi and taxi driver licenses.

2.   The suspension or revocation of taxi and taxi driver licenses.

3.   Reconsideration under section 17 of the 1985 Transport Act of decisions made in respect of specific taxi and taxi driver licenses or applications for licenses.

4.   The issue of 'unfit' notices.

5.   The appointment of taxi ranks.

On the rare occasion that, in the public interest, a very urgent decision is required in the absence of the Head of the PCO, a TfL director has delegated authority to suspend a driver's license. Responsibility for conducting personal hearings under section 17(4) of the 1985 Transport Act is delegated to the Head of the PCO or other such person appointed by him for that purpose. All decisions made by the Head of the PCO regarding specific licenses remain subject to appeal under the relevant statutory provisions.

We come now to the 'Knowledge'. I must say at the outset that the provision of information for a would be 'Knowledge boy' exceeds any which existed when I started the 'Knowledge' in April 1955. With regard to the new testing system the intention was to introduce an IT element while still retaining the "one to one" interview. The idea was sound enough, a constant level of service and an objective assessment of the topographical knowledge for the candidates.

At first there were problems, mainly a difficulty in the recruitment and retaining Knowledge of London Examiners, to meet the increased number of candidates appearances, this resulted, and here the PCO are quite candid; "In appointments increasing to unacceptable levels." Which meant that it was taking longer to get through the 'Knowledge'.

That problem has now been overcome following the introduction of higher rates of pay, and the introduction of flexible working arrangements. There is also the issue of the topographical knowledge requirement for private hire car drivers,' though it does seem that a computer system can be used for testing those licensees if required. In the long term there is of course the possible implementation for the 'knowledge' via GPS/GIS systems to be considered.

THE NEW BLUE BOOK INTRODUCED

Following a review of the Knowledge of London testing process, the 'Blue Book' runs have been considerably reduced from 468 runs in the old blue books to 320 in the current version. It now lists 30 types of points such as police stations, cinemas, theatres, government offices, Coroners Courts, prisons, and places of interest etc. It is very comprehensive and it does have a blue cover.

A lot of thought has gone into the design and content of this new 'blue book'. It explains exactly what has to be done, the equipment necessary to learn the knowledge. It deals with answering questions at the PCO, how to do the runs and what to look for, the Suburban knowledge and advice on attending the PCO.

The candidate is told exactly how to do the knowledge, advising on a 'call over' partner, in fact all that is required to commence learning the 'knowledge' of an area within a six mile radius of Charing Cross. There is also information as to how to do the Suburbs once a candidate obtained his requisition.

THE RUNS

Yes, it is still there at No.1, Manor House Station to Gibson Square, as it was in 1955 and many years previously. The difference though is in all the runs which come after. From Gibson Square it is on to Thornhill Square for the start of the next run to Queens Square and thence from Chancery Lane Station to Rolls Road SE1. Then from Pages Walk to St Martins Theatre WC2. The amount of time and effort saved is immediately plain to see. So it carries on throughout the 320 runs.

THE SUBURBS

The New Blue Book even tells you how to do the suburbs. It even lists a route such as The White City to Uxbridge. It shows a line route of the A40 and also shows the turn off points to other places such as North Hillingdon or Ruislip with their respective road numbers. It looks so easy I might consider applying to get my license back. Yes guv?. LAP? no problem leave on the left in Piccadilly, forward Knightsbridge via the HPC underpass   forward Brompton Road, forward Thurloe Place, forward Cromwell Road........ ... .

END PIECE

Some years ago when private hire cars were first licensed outside London from 1976, the taxi radio circuits vowed that they would never accept private hire cars on their circuits. Today it is the rule rather than the exception. They have had to accept private hire cars simply to survive, engulfed as they are by thousands of private hire cars.

I am convinced that eventually it will happen in London as more and more customers, especially the corporate clients desert the taxi circuits for a licensed private hire car who will offer a far better service, and greater reliability because of their numbers, at a fare at least 25 per cent lower than radio taxis charge. They will operate comfortable cars and they will not refuse to take someone south of the river!

I only hope that what I have uncovered will be taken up and acted upon, but why do I have this feeling that it will not and that I will have to suffer a range of insulting remarks? Of one thing I am convinced, the blame for what the trade is facing must lay at the door of those 'rednecks' who have campaigned long and hard for the number of drivers to be curtailed, without any thought for the future.

Appendix 1   DETAILS OF CABS AND DRIVERS

Year	Cabs Lic.	Hansoms	Growlers	New Cabs	Drivers	Per Cab
1869	7,542	N/G	N/G	N/G	N/G	N/G*
1870	7,341	"	"	"	"	
1871	7,818	"		"	"	"
1872	8,160	"		"	"	"
1873	9,655	"		"	" "	"
1874	Details of cabs were not given in this years report					
1875	Only the number of new drivers were given - 300					
1876	Only number of new cabs were given - 400					
1877	8,529	4,535	3,994	760	10,760	1.26
1878	8,981	4,877	4,014	-	11,123	1.24
1879	9,210	5,065	4,145	-	11,667	1.27
1880	NIG	-	-	-	12,654	1.12
1881*	9,647	5,800	3,847	437	12,630	1.30
1882	9,982	-		1,204	13,007	0.13
1883	10,381	6,579	3,802	1,192	13,534	1.30
1884	10,569	6,832	3,737	1,244	13,824	1.31
1885	10,874	6,877	3,997	1,207	14,252	1.31
1886	11,017	7,020	3,997	1,524	14,852	1.35
1887	11,246	7,219	4,027	-	15,100	1.34
1888	11,409	N/G	N/G	N/G	N/G	-
1889	11,375	7,409	3,966	896	15,513	1.36
1890	11,297	7,376	3,921	N/G	15,336	1.36
1891	11,129	7,320	3,809	N/G	15,219	1.37
1892	10,812	7,133	3,679	N/G	15,011	1.39
1893	10,806	7,193	3,613	758	14,985	1.39
1894	10,897	7,268	3,629	463	14,672	1.35
1895	10,961	7,425	3,536	513	13,498	1.23
1896	11,034	7,585	3,449	N/G	13,623	1.23
1897	11,508	7,925	3,583	1,114	13,673	1.19
1898	11,547	7,899	3,648	988	13,475**	1.17
1899	No report traced dealing with vehicles					
1900	11,252	7,531	3,721	N/G	13,201	1.17

N/G = Not given in Commissioner's Report

The Commissioner's Report of 1881 referred for the first time to the Public Carriage - Licensing Branch with cabs identified as a separate entity in the report..

In the same year the Lost Property Office was transferred from Great Scotland Yard to 21 Whitehall Place. Apparently the move proved satisfactory, giving as it did, more room for the licensing branch.

Although the earlier Commissioner' s Reports showed some inconsistencies, never-the-less it does not affect the general conclusions.

Appendix 2

Year	Cabs Lic.	Hansoms	Growlers	N Cabs	Drivers N	Drivers H
1901	11,170	7,454	3,719	N/G	N/G	N/G
1902	11,382	7,577	3,805	N/G	N/G	N/G1903	11,405	7,499

1903			3,906	1		1	13,469	
1904	11,059	7,135	3,922	2		2	N/G	
1905	10,931	6,996	3,935	19		23	12,663	
1906	10,492	6,648	3,844	96		124	12,343	
1907	10,541	5,942	3,866	723		N/G	N/G	
1908	11,280	4,826	3,649	2,805		N/G	12,406	
1909	No Commissioners Report found for 1909							
1910	15,995	N/G	N/G	N/G	5,838		N/G	
1911	No reference to vehicles or drivers							
1912	No Commissioners Report found for 1912							
1913	11,862	N/G	N/G	N/G	9,057		2,805	
1914	No Commissioners Report found for 1914							
1915	No Commissioners Report found for 1915							
1916	Nothing relating to cabs in this Report							
1917	Nothing relating to cabs in this Report							
1918	5,978	N/G	N/G		5,451		N/G	527
1919	N/G	N/G	N/G		N/G		9,399	N/G
1920	6,546	N/G	N/G		N/G		N/G	N/G
1921	Nothing relating to cabs in this report							
1922	7,581	N/G	N/G		7,191		N/G	390
1923	Hansoms & Growlers*				8,021		N/G	347
1924	8,323	"		"	N/G		N/G	280
1925	8,481	"		"	N/G		10,537	223
1926	8,686	"		"	8,478		10,686	186
1927	8,147	"		"	7,997		10,269	150
1928	No Commissioners Report found							
1929	7,947	"	"				10,742	87
1930	7,860	"		"	7,860		10,632	87
1931	8,103	"		"	8,152		11,080	69
1932	8,121	"		"	8,074		11,347	54
1933	8,025	"		"	7,995		11,461	30
1934	8,193	"		"	8,181		11,488	22
1935	8,160	"		"	8,180		11,587	20
1936	8,061	"		"	8,078		11,520	23
1937	8,057	"		"	8,044		11,636	13
1938	7,779	"		"	7,893		11,655	12
1939	6,691	"		"	6,683		11,404	8
	There were no Reports for 1940/1/2							
1943	5,604							2
1944	7,768							4
1945	5,321							
1946	5,855	269	drivers were licensed				8,377	2
1947	6,079						8,392	2
1948	6,149						8,509	
1949	6,965	2	cabs fitted with radio				9,101	
1950	7,129	7	cabs fitted with radio				x 9,623	

Appendix 3

Year	Cabs	Lic Drivers	Radio cabs	0/Drivers	Ratio Drs/cabs
1951	6,194*	9,278	180	N/G	1.50
1952	5,437	9,134	439	2,406	1.68
1953	5,609	9,077	552	N/G	1.62
1954	5,553	9,039	748	N/G	1.63
1955	5,897	9,015	974	2,625	1.53
1956	5,898	9,051	1,00	N/G	1.53
1957	6,118	9,195	1,046	2,612	1.50
1958	6,157	9,362	N/G	2,616	1.52
1959		No Report traced for 1959			
1960	6,651	11,026	N/G	2,733	1.63
1961	6,776	10,691	766	2,814	1.58
1962	7,008	10,404	759	2,919	1.48
1963	7,372	10,867	696	3,101	1.47
1964	7,669	11,071	710	3,339	1.44
1965	7,390	11,534	718	3,391	1.56
1966	N/G	11,872	N/G	N/G	-
1967	7,832	12,140	813	3,636	1.55
1968		No Report traced for 1968			
1969	8,412	12,776	885	3,736	1.52
1970	8,652	13,291	963	N/G	1.54
1971	9,586	13,819	1,048	N/G	1.42
1972	10,145	14,535	1,085	5,068	1.43
1973	10,406	15,238	1,347	4,992	1.46
1974	11,021	15,699	1,797	5,746	1.42
1975	11,260	16,037	2,223	6,129	1.42
1976	11,838	16,152	2,291	6,556	1.36
1977*	12,452	16,474	2,577	7,464	1.32
1978	12,453	16,740	2,684	7,701	1.36
1979	12,267	17,076	2,861	7,643	1.39
1980	12,385	17,377	2,960	7,592	1.40
198k	12,560	17,825	3,299	7,936	1.42
1982	12,809	18,086	3,340	8,050	1.41
1983	13,127	18,205	3,816	8,346	1.39
1984	13,574	18,421	4,115	8,577	1.36
1985	13,775	18,649	4,769	8,654	1.35
1986,	14,676	19,186	5,338	8,702	1.31
1987	14,792	19,685	6,045	N/G	1.33
1988		No details of drivers etc in this Report			
1989	15,622	20,522	6,659	wheelchair cabs 2,052	
1990	16,190	20,926	7,025	" " " 3,952	
1991	16,529	20,468	6,824	" " " 5,322	
1992	N/G	20,468	N/G	N/G N/G N/G	
1993	"	20,483	"	" " " "	
1994	"	21,357	"	" " " "	
1995	"	21,584	"	" " " "	
1996	"	22,109	"	" " " "	
1997	"	22,252	"	" " " "	

DETAILS OF THE KNOWLEDGE OF LONDON

YEAR	APPLICANTS	PASSED	FAILED	EXAMS	GREEN BADGE	YELLOW BG
1869- 1883 NO RECORDS						
1884	1,931	1,214	717	-	ALL	-
1885	1,830	1,219	611	-	ALL	-
1886	1,873	1,328	545	-	ALL	-
1887	1,936	1,357	579	-	ALL	-
1888	2,316	1,461	855	-	ALL	-
1890	-	1,642	-	-	ALL	-
1891	-	1,119	-	-	ALL	-
1892	-	1,050	-	-	ALL	-
1893	-	1,168	-	-	ALL	-
1894	1,205	854	351	-	ALL	-
1895	857	616	241	-	ALL	-
1896	1,645	1,058	587	-	ALL	-
1897	1,952	971	981	-	ALL	-
1898	-	776		-	-	ALL
1899	-	971		-	-	ALL
1900	918	638	280	-	ALL	-
1901	No details of the knowledge in this Report					
1902	1,072	837	235	-	ALL	
1903	1,039	805	234	-	ALL	
1904	735	360	375	-	ALL	
1905	682	331	351	-	ALL	
1906	578	302	276	-	ALL	
1907	No details of the knowledge in this Report					
1908	3,142	771	2,371	-	ALL	
1909	No details of the knowledge in this Report					
1910	2,052	598	1,454	-	ALL	
1911	1,722	927	795	-	ALL	
1912	No Report traced			-		
1913	676	366	310	-	ALL	
1914	No Report traced					
1915	No Report traced					
	No details of the knowledge in this Report					
1916	No details of the knowledge in this Report					

DETAILS OF THE KNOWLEDGE OF LONDON

Year	Applied	Pass	N/Pass	Exams	G.badge	Y.badge	Sub/Lond
1917	No details of the knowledge in this Report						
1918	No details of the knowledge in this Report						
1919	No details other than four women were licensed						
1920	No details of the knowledge in this Report						
1921	No details of the knowledge in this Report						
1922	No details of the knowledge in this Report						
1923	N/G	301	N/G	8,154	All	N/G	N/G
1924	"	355	"	N/G	All	"	"
1925	"	737	"	10,195	All	"	"
1926	"	474	"	9,481	All	"	"
1927	"	305	"	7,503	All	"	"
1928		No Report found			All	"	"
1929*	"	491		13,701	All	"	"
1930	"	540	"	18,365	All	"	"
1931	"	468	"	21,121	All	"	"
1932	"	588	"	N/G	All	"	"
1933	1,108	434		674	All	"	"
1934	No details of the knowledge in this report						
1935	"	438	"	"	All	"	"
1936	"	461	"	"	All	"	"
1937	"	418	N/G	13,644	All	"	"
1938	1,076	374	702	9,268	All	"	"
1939	No details of the knowledge in this report						
1940	No Report found						
1941	No Report found						
1942	No Report found						
1943	No details of the knowledge in this Report						
1944	No details of the knowledge in this Report						
1945	N/G	51	N/G	N/G	All	"	"
1946	4,231	106	"	"	All	"	"
1947	648	232	"	"	All	"	"
1948	1,041	341	673	9,554	All	"	"
1949	1,113	570	568	11,821	463	107	"
1950	1,220	59	626	13,276	507	87	"
1951	725	508	217	11,348	466	42	"
1952	343	151	91	6,401	219	23	"
1953	356	135	235	4,386	107	28	"
1954	474	149	325	5,090	125	24	"
1955	No details of the knowledge in this Report						
1956	631	330	301	7,938	291	39	"
1957	843	388	455	9,161	383	5	"
1958	1,164	518	646	12,125	454	64	"
1959		No Report found					
1960	898	667	231	14,289	599	68	"

*The Commissioner of Police blamed the high numbers failing was due to insufficient knowledge

DETAILS OF THE KNOWLEDGE OF LONDON

Year	Applied	Pass	N/Pass	Exams	G.Bdg	Y.Bdg.	Sub/Lon
1961	825	594	231	11,095	760	65	"
1962	1,350	498	852	12,380	433	65	"
1963	1,531	648	883	16,448	514	114	20
1964	1,440	686	774	18,461	561	105	20
1965	1,349	671	678	16,855	546	105	20
1966	1,254	741	539	16,315	618	97	26
1967	1,446	721	725	15,043	619	102	37
1968	1,627	613	1,014	NG	504	109	18
1969	2,199	871	1,328	29,708	759	112	37
1970	2,276	951	1,325	23,076	800	151	42
1971	2,827	982	1,807	25,470	830	152	38
1972	2,605	1,159	1,446	27,202	993	166	47
1973	1,835	1,188	647	25,871	1,054	134	63
1974	1,732	952	780	20,968	837	115	53
1975	2,224	839	1,405	19,145	692	147	38
1976	2,938	588	2,359	19,869	467	121	18
1977	3,201	729	2,472	21,008	606	123	35
1978			No Report found				
1979	1,636	725	N/G	NIG	N/G	N/G	30
1980	2,118	659	1,459	20,808	659	N/G	30
1981	2,286	790	1,496	16,154	613	177	21
1982	2,736	623	2.113	11,730	484	138	21
1983	3,647	633	3,014	13,899	498	135	41
1984	4,660	557	4,103	17,826	521	36	44
1985	4,878	731	4,147	14,214	700	31	43
1986	2,190	901	1,289	15,340	876	25	42
1987	2,542	713	1,641	15,340	694	19	20
1988	2,641	748	1,893	14,862	737	11	15
1989	3,736	785	2,891	13,152	785	30	19
1990	3,821	705	3,294	16,313	527	178	1
1991	3,142	1,149	2,285	19,832	857	292	0
1992	3,662	830	2,832	N/G	770	60	
1993	2,357	674	1,683	N/G	634	"	"
1994	4,186	672	3,814	N/G	660	12	0
1995	2,925	622	2,152	N/G	600	22	0
1996	3,357	697	3,764	N/G	575	122	25
1997	4,107	603	3,150	N/G	425	188	11

The Metropolitan Police Reports run from January to December
and published in June the following year.
To avoid any confusion the figures in the far right column
under the heading Sub/Lon (Suburban to London) are not part of
the overall increase of drivers doing the 'knowledge', because
they are already licensed drivers in the trade and cannot be
counted as new drivers.

PROGRESS OF RADIO CABS AND OWNER DRIVERS RECORDS BOTH COMMENCED IN
1949

Year	Radio Cabs			Owner Drivers	
1949	2			NG*	
1950	7			2,726	
1951	180			2,566	
1952	439	inc. 24	sub.	2,406	
1953	552			NG	
1954	748			NG	
1955	974			2,626	
1956	1,005			2,612	
1957	1,046			NG	
1958	NG*			2,616	
1959	NC			NG	
1960	NC			2,733	
1961	766			2,814	
1962	759			2,919	
1963	696			3,101	
1964	710	inc.113	Sub.	3,399	
1965	718			3,391	
1966	NC			NG	
1967	813	inc.108	Sub.	3,636	
1968	901			NG	
1969	885			3,736	
1970	963	inc. 91	Sub.	NG	
1971	1,048			3,068	
1972	1,085			NG	
1973	1,347			4,992	
1974	1,797			5,746	
1975	2,223			6,129	
1976	2,291			6,556	
1977	2,577			7,464	
1978	No Report found				
1979	2,861			7,643	
1980	2,960			7,592	
1981	3,299			7,936	
1982	3,340			8,050	
1983	3,816			8,346	
1984	4,115			8,577	60%
1985	4,769			8,654	
1986	5,338			8,702	
1987	6,045			NG	
1988	No Report found				
1989	6,569			NG	
1990	7,025			NG	
1991	6,824			NG	

No Commissioner of Police Reports available from 1992 to date1998.
*Not Given

A series I Morris-Oxford of 1946, the first new cab to be introduced in London after the war and the first cab to have a fully enclosed driver's door.

A Carbodies Austin Fx3 introduced in 1948. Seen here to advantage outside Buckingham Palace in that year.

Above: Some of the boys on their bikes in the days before the knowledge was done on mopeds and below... learning some of the runs

PUBLIC CARRIAGES.

NOTICE

TO

DRIVERS AND CONDUCTORS

The attention of Drivers and Conductors, on obtaining a Licence, is specially directed to the Law which requires—

 1. That the Badge is to be worn conspicuously on the breast by each licensed Driver or Conductor at all times during his employment, whether such Driver or Conductor be Proprietor or not. The Penalty for neglecting to do so is **FORTY SHILLINGS.**

2. That within Two Days of every Change of abode, the Licence and Copy are to be produced at the Public Carriage Office for the New Address to be endorsed thereon and properly registered.

NOTE.—THE LICENCE AND COPY MAY BE SENT BY POST, PROVIDED A WRITTEN NOTICE OF THE CHANGE OF ABODE, SIGNED BY THE DRIVER OR CONDUCTOR, BE SENT WITH IT.

3. That all Property left in a Cab or Stage Carriage be deposited at the nearest Police Station within 24 hours.

And—
4. That the Licence, Copy and Badge are to be returned to the Commissioner of Police within Three Days after the expiration of the Licence under a Penalty of £5. They may be handed in at any Police Station, or may be sent by Post direct to the Public Carriage Office.

Drivers of Cabs are also reminded that the guard rail and chain or other means provided on Cabs should on all occasions be used to secure luggage.

Drivers and Conductors are also informed that Returns of all Convictions are received from the Courts and registered against them at this office, and that such Convictions will be considered before another Licence is granted.

BYNG OF VIMY,
The Commissioner of Police of the Metropolis.

METROPOLITAN POLICE OFFICE,
NEW SCOTLAND YARD, S.W. 1.
26th April, 1930.

[C.A. 78969]